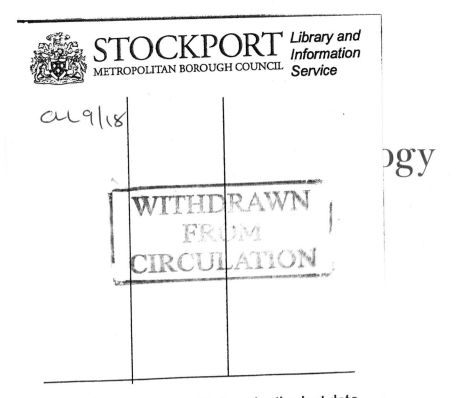
ogy

Please return/renew this item by the last date
shown.
Books may also be renewed by phone or the
Internet

TEL: 0161 217 6009
www.stockport.gov.uk/libraries

The Victorian Society

Studies in Victorian Architecture and Design

Volume Four

Ecclesiology Abroad

The British Empire and Beyond

Edited by G. A. Bremner

London · 2012

The Victorian Society is the champion for Victorian and Edwardian architecture and related arts in England and Wales.
Lectures, walks and tours are organised for members, who also receive this journal and *The Victorian,* our thrice-yearly magazine. For information contact: The Victorian Society, 1 Priory Gardens, London W4 1TT

www.victoriansociety.org.uk

ISBN 978–0–901657–53–4
ISSN 1756–6460

Designed and typeset in Kepler by Dalrymple
Printed by Nicholson & Bass, Belfast

Front cover: St Mary's Pro Cathedral, Auckland, by Benjamin Mountfort, 1886–98 [Art History & Theory Visual Resources Collection, University of Canterbury].

Back cover: Mahone Bay, Nova Scotia [Peter Coffman].

Frontispiece: Detail from view of a prefabricated iron church for Melbourne as it appeared in Hemming's manufactory yard, Bristol, 1853 [State Library of Victoria].

The publication of this volume of *Studies in Victorian architecture and design* is dedicated in memory of Colin Cunningham (1942–2011), a great friend of the Victorian Society.

Ecclesiology Abroad

STUDIES IN VICTORIAN ARCHITECTURE AND DESIGN · VOLUME 4

1 · Introduction: Victorian Architecture – an Expanded Field

ALEX BREMNER

The collection of essays that comprise this volume of *Studies in Victorian Architecture and Design* were originally presented in 2010 at the Victorian Society's annual symposium, on that occasion entitled 'Ecclesiology and Empire: Victorian Church Design Outside the British Isles, 1830–1910'.[1] The intention was not only to showcase current research in the field, but also to remind the predominantly British audience of the sheer geographical extent of 'Victorian' architecture, albeit with respect to a single building typology: churches.

The global spread of Victorian architecture is undoubtedly known and appreciated, but is perhaps not discussed as often as it ought to be. The Victorian age was of course noted for being an imperial one, and Queen Victoria herself was monarch of a 'Greater Britain' that stretched around the world. It is nearly always illuminating to consider 'home' developments in light of 'colonial' happenings, for many of the architects involved in designing buildings for various parts of Britain's empire were also leading figures on the British scene, including A.W.N. Pugin, G.G. Scott, William Butterfield, G.F. Bodley, William White, G.E. Street and William Burges, to name but a few [fig. 1.2]. In this respect, the symposium attempted to cover as much 'territory' as possible, including as many noted designers as was feasible, giving if not a comprehensive account of ecclesiological practices abroad, then at least offering a reasonable snapshot of the nature and extent of activity.

One of the unfortunate drawbacks of the one-day symposium format is that it forced the organisers to focus primarily on only one aspect of the Victorian architectural experience abroad, namely the empire. Many of the impressive churches designed by noted Victorian architects in mainland Europe, for example, in places such as Paris and Rome, necessarily had to be omitted. An anomaly with this imperial agenda, however, was that it included discussion of the United States. America was of course no longer part of Britain's global empire during the Victorian era, but it was felt by the organisers, by way of comparison, that some analysis of the American scene would be useful to gain a better perspective on the circulation of architectural ideas around the British world. This is important, not least because some of the architects that ended up in locations such as Australia, New Zealand and Canada received their professional training in the

Fig 1.1 | Interior of St Paul's Anglican cathedral, Melbourne, Australia (1880–91), original design by William Butterfield [St Paul's Cathedral].

United States, not Britain. One that readily springs to mind is John Horbury Hunt (1838–1904), who came to Sydney in 1863 aged 25 via the office of Edward C. Cabot in Boston. For the purposes of this volume reference to the term 'empire' in the principal title has therefore been omitted, opting instead for the more catholic phrase 'Ecclesiology Abroad'.

Despite these limitations, it is hoped that this will form the first part in a series of symposia and edited volumes produced by the Victorian Society that will deal with ecclesiology (and Victorian architecture in general) beyond the British Isles, including that in mainland Europe. The following introduction, the essence of which was presented at the opening of the symposium, is intended as an encouragement to all of us interested in the study and preservation of Victorian buildings to think more broadly about the possibilities of 'Victorian architecture'.

RECONSIDERING THE LIMITS OF AN ARCHITECTURAL CATEGORY

Victorian architecture has always been an expansive if not problematic category. Having spent many years of my life in Australia, I am very much aware of the Victorian heritage of that country, especially the State in which I lived (the State of Victoria, no less) and, in particular, the city of Melbourne ('Marvellous Melbourne'), a city replete with Victorian buildings, including the magnificent St Paul's cathedral by William Butterfield [fig. 1.1]. At the same time, however, I am acutely conscious of what the noted Australian historian Geoffrey Blainey once described as the 'tyranny of distance'[2] – that in Australia could be found a peculiar building stock that linked the city, the State, and the country, in a very explicit and obvious way, to a place, namely Britain, over 10,000 miles away. This building stock, this architecture, was quite obviously *Victorian*.

Architecture of this kind was a manifestation or consequence of a much larger social, cultural, economic and political phenomenon at the time known as the British Empire – a phenomenon that was once described by the eminent Cambridge historian, John Robert Seeley, as the 'great fact' of modern English history.[3] It is always useful to remind ourselves of this fact, a fact that was brought to our attention by Asa Briggs, among others, nearly fifty years ago in his book *Victorian Cities*, which had a chapter dedicated to the city of Melbourne.[4] When we talk about Victorian architecture we are therefore talking about more than what was designed and built in Britain, but what was built in much of the known world at that time. As the essays collected in this volume illustrate, we see this not only in Australia but also in New Zealand, India, Africa and North America – indeed, in any place that was part of Brain's former empire, and, in some cases, outside it. 'Victorian architecture' therefore implies a kind of spectrum: a series of styles, movements and ideological currents in architecture that varied according to time and place but nevertheless carried within them certain identifiable traits that give Victorian architecture its peculiar character and that allows us to label it as such. In other words, there is no one Victorian architecture, but many.

Lending credence to this view is the fact that the variations one finds in such

Fig 1.2 | All Saints Anglican cathedral, Allahabad, India
(1870–87), by William Emerson [Alex Bremner]

architecture in other parts of the world are, it can be argued, no more or less marked than those one might encounter within Britain itself, in places as distant and diverse as Inverness, Manchester, Norwich, London, Bristol and Exeter. Victorian architecture is a very rich, multivalent and therefore widely geographical phenomenon, and should be celebrated for precisely that reason. The difficulties and pressures that face the Victorian building stock in this country also faces that in other countries, in some cases much more so. This is something that Ian Lochhead has discovered with devastating force recently in Christchurch, New

Zealand, during the awful series of earthquakes that rocked that city in 2010 and 2011 [fig. 1.3].[5]

We therefore need to talk about Victorian architecture not just in a detailed, local way but also in a much *bigger*, global way, promoting and celebrating the *world* of Victorian architecture. This is necessary for academic no less than practical reasons.

The intention of the essays collected here, therefore, is to suggest that there is a real opportunity to connect and bring into a more meaningful dialogue the macro and micro worlds of Victorian architecture, whether we are talking about materials, construction techniques or stylistic influences. Such an outlook dovetails precisely with larger intellectual currents in the cognate disciplines of history, economics and the social sciences. As we now live in a thoroughly globalised world, this has given historians pause for thought, and, in a way, forced them to rethink the cultural and political dimensions of history and the way it is written. In the past decade or so we have seen the emergence of historical concepts and categories such as 'Atlantic History', 'Pacific History' and latterly 'World/Global History', all devised in an attempt to draw wider associations and connections between what were hitherto understood as discrete or exceptional historical phenomena. This research initiative has been concerned with the interconnectedness of objects and events though time and space, especially through the agency of empire.

So why did the more expansive outlook of historians such as Seeley disappear in Britain? It is a complex story, suffice to say here that there was of course a narrowing of horizons as Britain witnessed the dismantling of its colonial empire after the Second World War, the loss of its former position of global dominance, and its subsumption into the European idea, and all of this against the backdrop of the Cold War and the advent of NATO. These factors, it has been argued, led to a certain 'myopia' in the way the history of Britain came to be studied, understood and written about, witnessing a return to the so-called 'little England' view.

This is important because we are now emerging (in fact, have emerged) on the other side of this period of geographic contraction into a perspective that no longer views empire as an embarrassment to be downplayed or brushed under the carpet, but one that must be confronted, acknowledged and dealt with in a serious and systematic way. The origins of this new perspective date back to a series of ground-breaking articles published between 1974 and 1982 by the New Zealand-born historian J.G.A. Pocock, in which he sought to redefine what was meant by the term 'British history'. Pocock's initial observations led to the conclusion that there was nothing that could properly be described as 'British history', and that what generally passed for the history of Britain, or the British Isles, was in fact the history of England.[6] In his opening salvo, 'British History: A Plea for a New Subject', published in the *New Zealand Journal of History* in 1974, Pocock noted of this problem that 'when one considers what "Britain" means – that it is the name of a realm inhabited by two, and more than two, nations, whose history

Fig 1.3 | Remains of the Presbyterian church, Lyttelton, New Zealand (1864–5), by Samuel Farr, after the earthquake of 2011 [Ian Lochhead].

has been expansive to the extent of planting settlements and founding derivative cultures beyond the Four Seas – it is evident that the history of this complex expression has never been seriously attempted.'[7] In short, Pocock's principal contention was that 'British history', in its most *plural* and *comprehensive* sense, was an 'unknown' subject.

Clearly, from where Pocock was standing, 'British history' was not only something different from the history of England, but also something far more expansive, both geographically and historiographically. This included not only English political and cultural expansion and domination within the British Isles – what Pocock refers to as the Anglo-Norman transformation of the Atlantic Archipelago – but also expansion beyond this into North America, India, Australasia and Africa. This was Pocock's challenge to the modern historian: that one can 'conceive of "British history" no longer as being an archipelagic or even an Atlantic-American phenomenon, but as having occurred on a planetary scale.' [8]

As architecture is one of the most immediate and conspicuous forms of cultural production, Pocock's approach and the insights it offers has much to recommend to the study of architecture broadly conceived, and might just as easily apply to 'British architecture' as it does to 'British history'.[9]

Christianity was of course a major social force in British culture during the Victorian period. As Theodore Hoppen has observed, never was Britain more religious than at this time in its history.[10] With this in mind, the current volume attempts to achieve two things: firstly, to situate and, indeed, to stimulate our understanding of what constitutes Victorian architecture in a much wider but no less authentic context; and secondly to shed light upon a significant aspect of it, namely Christianity: a facet of British imperial expansion that is often overlooked. This second aspect in particular has occurred to me most recently in my own research on this topic, revealing how many of the architects and clergymen (and their sponsors) associated with the Anglican missionary cause worldwide were closely related, either through family ties, social and political connections, educational background or professional networks.[11] Nearly all were interested to some degree or other in architecture and the role it played in the growth and consolidation of Anglican discipline and spirituality worldwide.[12] It is now clear that the organisation and maintenance of these connections reveal Britain and its empire to have been a continuous field of Anglican activity and agency, not as a series of fragmented or wholly isolated spheres of influence.[13]

The essays in this volume will therefore traverse all four quarters of the globe, looking at the activities of Anglican, Catholic, Presbyterian and Nonconformist cultures alike in their attempts to respond to the rise of the Gothic Revival and the dictates of ecclesiology. We will see everything from the most 'primitive' to the most refined responses to the particular demands of ecclesiastical architecture in the Australasian context; the response (or not) to climate in Asia and Canada; ideas of continuity and change in Africa; and how these ideas also carried weight in the United States. It is hoped that in all of this, despite the apparent differences, those distinct and identifiable traits that connect Victorian architecture, in all of its guises, the world over, will remain clearly identifiable.

NOTES

1. The symposium took place at the Art Workers' Guild, London, on 6 November 2010. The only author in the current volume not present that day was Desmond Martin. I would also like to take this opportunity to thank Ian Dungavell and David Glasper for their editorial assistance, without which this volume would not have been possible.

2. Geoffrey Blainey, *The Tyranny of Distance: How Distance Shaped Australia's History*, Melbourne, 1966.

3. J.R. Seeley, *The Expansion of England*, London, 1883, p.12.

4. A. Briggs, *Victorian Cities*, Harmondsworth, 1968, pp.277–310.

5. Since the earthquakes in Christchurch, G.G. Scott's magnificent cathedral in that city has faced repeated attempts on the part of local and national governments, as well as the Anglican Church in New Zealand, to have it completely demolished, despite the fact that it can be salvaged. The Victorian Society has done its part in writing to the New Zealand government to register its concern over the cathedral and to protest at its scheduled demolition. Ian Lochhead and others, including this author, continue to protest against the cathedral's demolition.

6. J.G.A. Pocock, 'The Limits and Divisions of British History', *Studies in Public Policy*, no. 31 (University of Strathclyde, 1979), p.7.

7. J.G.A. Pocock, 'British History: A Plea for a New Subject', *New Zealand Journal of History*, vol. 8:1 (1974), p.5.

8. J.G.A. Pocock, 'The Limits and Divisions of British History: In Search of the Unknown Subject', *American Historical Review*, vol. 87:2 (1982), p.319. Here Pocock also observes that: '"British history," both cultural and political, is discovered to have exceeded even the archipelagic and Atlantic dimension and to have established itself in a number of areas in the southern hemisphere. The history of these settler nations … makes a claim to be considered part of "British history" and to enlarge the meaning of that term.' For the same argument in a related context, see J.G.A. Pocock, 'The New British History in Atlantic Perspective: An Antipodean Commentary', *American Historical Review*, vol. 104:2 (1999), pp.490–500.

9. In fact, as C.A. Bayly has noted, a global perspective on modern history must also include the numerous forms of cultural practice and production, including architecture. See: C.A. Bayly, *Birth of the Modern World*, Oxford, 2003, pp. 1, 384–5.

10. K. T. Hoppen, *The Mid-Victorian Generation 1846–1886*, Oxford, 2000, p.427.

11. For example: Howard Le Couteur, 'Using the "Old Boys" Network: Bishop Tufnell's Search for Men and Money', paper delivered at the Australian Historical Association conference, Hobart (1998); Austin Cooper, 'Forgotten Australian Anglican: Edward Coleridge', *Pacifica*, vol. 3 (1990), pp.257–67.

12. Many colonial clergymen were members and patrons of the two influential university architectural societies (Cambridge Camden Society and the Oxford Architectural Society).

13. For the results of this research, see my forthcoming book *Imperial Gothic: Religious Architecture and High Anglican Culture in the British Empire, c.1840–70*, to be published by Yale University Press in Spring 2013.

✠ Ill.^{mus} R.^{mus} Robertus Gul. Willson.

I. Episc. Hobarton.   Alumnus Huius Coll.

2 · 'Solemn Chancels and Cross Crowned Spires': Pugin's Antipodean Vision and its Implementation

BRIAN ANDREWS

> *Think of everything you can for Bishop Willson. It is a good work in which he is engaged.*[1]

These encouraging words were penned by A.W.N. Pugin (1812–52) to his colleague and industrial partner John Hardman of Birmingham in November 1847, during a visit by his close friend Robert William Willson (1794–1866), first Bishop of Hobart Town, to his Ramsgate home in the course of a return visit to England from Tasmania. Pugin would recall Willson's endeavours again in September 1848 when penning a letter to *The Tablet* triggered by criticism of his stance *inter alia* on the essentiality of rood screens in Roman Catholic churches. He averred:

> *But while on the one hand we must deplore their disheartening attacks on the revival of Ecclesiastical solemnity, yet on the other, when we reflect on the immense progress that has been made in this respect within the space of a few years, we must be filled with thankfulness for the past, and animated with burning zeal for the future ... England is, indeed, awakened to a sense of her ancient glory, and the reverence for things speedily passes on to the men and principles which produced them. But why do I say England –Europe, Christendom is aroused; wherever I travel, I meet pious and learned ecclesiastics and laymen all breathing the same sentiments regarding mediaeval art, and more than one Bishop has departed across the ocean to the antipodes, carrying the seeds of Christian design to grow and flourish in the New World, and soon the solemn chancels and cross-crowned spires will arise, the last object which the mariner will behold on the shores of the Pacific till their venerable originals greet his glad view on England's shores.*[2]

Pugin was referring to John Bede Polding O S B, first Archbishop of Sydney, and to Willson. But while Polding's dealings with him were not essentially different from those of his English clients, both Anglican and Catholic, his relationship with Willson would result in what was arguably the most comprehensive attempt at realising the totality of his vision by perhaps the one clergyman who fully aligned himself with that ideal and did all within his limited financial means to implement it. That vision was for the bringing about of a revival of the Roman Catholic faith in England (and by extension its colonial possessions). Pugin's perception

Fig 2.1 | Robert William Willson (1794–1866), first Bishop of
Hobart Town, painted *c.*1854 by John Rogers Herbert RA

of his role in this was alluded to later in the abovementioned letter to *The Tablet* where he stated that: 'architecture is the barometer of faith; it is not the arch, the pinnacle, the pillar that profiteth, but the spirit which produces them; and the revival or decline of true Ecclesiastical architecture is commensurate with that of the true faith. It is for these reasons that we labour for its restoration, and not as a mere abstract question of art.' Thus, Pugin's labours to resuscitate the architectural, furnishing and decorative repertoire of the English Middle Ages were not an end in themselves but a means, he passionately believed, for bringing about the improvement of the moral, social and spiritual condition of his age.

Pugin's reasoning – in highly compressed form – could be expressed something like this. Architecture was both the outcome and the expression of a society and its values. The gradual development of ecclesiastical architecture and art, and in particular the planning of churches and the disposition of their furnishings, was liturgically and therefore theologically based, thus expressing and embodying in their elements and their symbolism the faith and moral values of Christianity. This process evolved through the Middle Ages, so that with an increasingly complete Christian society all architecture was itself the increasingly complete expression of Christian faith and doctrine. This is why Pugin always referred to the Gothic as Christian architecture. Because it was perceived by him to be the most perfect embodiment of faith and doctrine, it had the power to rekindle the faith and its associated moral values. Thus, for a Christian it was the only admissible style, and its value and efficacy were as valid in the nineteenth century as in the fourteenth. The Renaissance, with its introduction of pagan elements and symbols, was therefore seen as an assault on the theological truths and symbolism embodied in the Gothic, and thus not only a blasphemous intrusion, but also a dilution of that unity of faith and morals as expressed in Christian architecture. Hence the inevitable decline, which Pugin perceived, over the ensuing centuries.

For Pugin, the inescapable conclusion of this world view was that Gothic was a moral imperative and therefore completely non-negotiable. It also followed that if his beliefs were to be translated into reality he must revive all the medieval crafts. For in order to resurrect the full liturgical, sacramental, and devotional life of the medieval church, the design and manufacture of vestments, liturgical metalwork, tombstones, memorial brasses, stained glass, book illustrations and so on, was just as essential to his vision as was the design of churches themselves. This same vision also drove him to advocate the revival of plainchant. That Willson subscribed to this view is evident both in his actions and in his correspondence. Thus, he could express in a letter of 13 March 1851 to his friend and episcopal colleague James Alipius Goold OSA, Roman Catholic Bishop of Melbourne, on the eve of the latter's departure for Europe: 'I hope you will return a full length *middle-age* man – I am sure we can produce more real Catholic feeling, either in buildings, Church furniture, &c &c in the good old style of our forefathers, than in the modern taste, and fanciful notions ...'[3]

The younger brother of Edward James Willson – architect, writer and collaborator with both Pugin and his father – William had close ties with the Pugin family. Trained for the priesthood at Oscott College, he was ordained on 16 December 1824 and sent early in 1825 to the Nottingham Mission. His immediate circle of friends included the Hardman family, the Earl of Shrewsbury, Bishop Milner, Doctor (later Cardinal) Wiseman, John Lingard (priest and scholar with whom he corresponded on controversial and polemical issues) and Pugin. It seems possible that, as both priest and friend, he may have had some role through his brother in Pugin's conversion.

Willson would appear to have been the outstanding exception to Cardinal Manning's famous dictum that in all the great English humanitarian activity of the early nineteenth century there was no Catholic name.[4] During his nineteen years in Nottingham he distinguished himself through his unceasing labours for the physically and mentally ill, irrespective of creed, and even held a licence for a private lunatic asylum for Roman Catholics in his house. It is a telling comment on his admirable character that he enjoyed the respect and friendship of the Nottingham Borough magistrates – all Protestants – in an era not renowned for religious tolerance, and it was doubtless his remarkable successes on behalf of the flotsam and jetsam of Nottingham society which led to his being nominated by Polding early in 1842 for the new see of Hobart Town, embracing the whole of Van Diemen's Land (later re-named Tasmania), virtually an island prison.

Upon hearing of Willson's nomination the Nottingham mayor, town clerk, and magistrates wrote a petition to the Holy See begging that he not be removed from their midst, whilst one magistrate, Thomas Close, a friend of Willson, wrote an impassioned plea to Bishop Thomas Walsh, Vicar Apostolic of the Central District, imploring him to back the petition. Rome initially agreed to their request, much to Polding's consternation. However, several months later, after discussions between Willson, Polding and Fr (later Archbishop) William Bernard Ullathorne OSB, who had personal experience of the Australian mission, he accepted the nomination.

Pugin probably learnt of Willson's initial selection for Hobart Town during a visit to Nottingham on 1 April 1842 in connection with the erection of St Barnabas' Church (later Cathedral). In later years Willson recalled with fondness to a clerical colleague Pugin's reaction at the news: 'Poor Pugin ... rubbed his hands, and smiling, said with great energy: "only think, the right thing will find its way at the antipodes!"'[5] No wonder. Before him was 'an unique opportunity to fully realise his Gothic and Christian vision in a pristine land in concert with another soul whose views exactly corresponded with his own, a place where no pagan intrusions would be countenanced. Here there would be no exhausting battles for rood screens, no condemnations of vestments, no ignorance of the function of his churches, no conventicles masquerading as settings for the sacred mysteries.'[6] In the many meetings at Nottingham over the coming months there would be time to plan their shared vision not for one church or one set of furnishings, but for the total needs of a diocese and its people, an opportunity unique in Pugin's entire career. And Pugin would prepare all these designs at no cost. The faithful of Van Diemen's Land would be baptised in a Pugin font and attend Mass celebrated in a Pugin-designed and furnished church by a priest wearing Pugin vestments and using Pugin altar vessels. Then at life's end they would be buried in the shadow of a Pugin churchyard cross, their final resting place marked by a Pugin headstone.

On 28 October 1842, with a delighted Pugin present, Willson was consecrated in St Chad's Cathedral, Birmingham, at the hands of Polding assisted by Bishops Walsh and Wareing. His pastoral staff was the gift of the Earl of Shrewsbury, his pectoral cross was from Pugin, whilst his precious mitre and ring had been given by Thomas Close and his wife respectively. All had been made by Hardmans to Pugin's designs. [fig. 2.1]

Willson's understanding of what would confront him in Van Diemen's Land, and the concomitant challenges for Pugin in realising his vision (having previously enjoyed access to the highest quality craft and constructional skills), seem most likely to have been informed by Ullathorne's somewhat bleak views arising from his experience there. When Ullathorne had visited Van Diemen's Land in 1833 there was just one priest, Fr Philip Connolly, on the island, and the only chapel was attached to Connolly's residence *Killard* in Hobart Town. When Ullathorne arrived at the chapel to say his Mass he was left with the following impression:

> I went up to the chapel to my Mass. It was situated on a plot of several
> acres in a beautiful position, but was in a most disgraceful state. There
> was a tidy little house enough, but the floor of the chapel consisted of
> loose boards of the gum tree, with their sharp edges curled up and the
> planks moving with every tread. The altar was a frame of wood with a
> most filthy old black antependium and altar cloths. The rough plaster
> at the back was covered with black-glazed cotton put up at the death of
> George IV and covered with filth. The other inner walls were but the first
> rough plaster, covered with dirt. The two sides and under the altar were
> refuse holes for the household, old discarded hats, lime-wash buckets,
> mops, brooms, all sorts of disgraceful rubbish heaped up and thrown
> about there. The altar linen, long unwashed, was thickly stained with
> port wine. There were no steps to the altar, but the same loose planks
> that formed the entire floor, and no seats for the people. The chalice and
> ciborium were tarnished as black as ink.[7]

This description brings to mind Pugin's depiction of an Anglican chancel in his *Contrasts*, illustrating 'the effect of the destructive or Protestant principles'.[8] Things had not much changed for the better by the time of Willson's episcopal appointment. There were just three Roman Catholic churches on the island, which had a land mass almost as large as Ireland. In Hobart Town, St Joseph's Church, a rectangular Gothick box with western tower designed by the Presbyterian architect James Alexander Thomson, had been opened in 1841. In Richmond, a little to the north of Hobart, St John the Evangelist's, another Gothick box, this one from plans furnished to Polding by the Bath architect Henry Edmund Goodridge, had been completed in 1837. The third church was another St Joseph's, again Gothick and with the same form as its Hobart counterpart. It was located in Launceston in the north of the island.

In designing churches for Willson, Pugin was faced with a dilemma apparently based on Ullathorne's admittedly dated views, namely, that he could not rely on the customary craft and other skills being available; nor, it would seem, was there even the ability to read and interpret architectural drawings! Accordingly, he came up with a remarkable solution which would, like the whole Tasmanian venture, be unique in his career. The three church designs which he produced for Willson in 1843 would be constructed by copying detailed scale models, with the smaller more complex stone details – gable crosses, holy water stoups, piscinas or sacrariums – being locally copied from exemplar stonework carved in England. The task of constructing the models and of carving the exemplars was given to craftsmen in the employ of George Myers, Pugin's favoured builder. Interestingly, no such difficulties were envisaged in the supply of church and other designs to Archbishop Polding of New South Wales in 1842, who had received conventional architectural drawings.

In a letter to the Earl of Shrewsbury dated 30 January 1844, Pugin mentioned '*3 models of small churches* all to take to pieces with the roofs &c framed, simple buildings that can be easily erected,' adding with evident satisfaction: 'It is quite delightful to start in the good style at the antipodes. It is quite an honour.'[9] Pugin had first alluded to the use of models instead of drawings in a letter of 26 August 1843 to his Oxford Movement friend John Rouse Bloxam where he observed: 'I am going to send out Models of churches tombstones fonts altars & altar furniture tiles Glass &c &c to Hobart Town to start the good style in the antipodes.'[10] It is clear that the models were both accurate and detailed, for George Myers' records reveal that they took a total of forty-eight days.[11] They were likely constructed to a scale of a half inch to the foot. This would have made them manageable as part of Willson's ship cargo, but it would have also rendered detail on furnishings to be constructed of wood, such as rood screens and sedilia, sufficiently large for accurate replication.

The liturgical basis for Pugin's Tasmanian church designs was the English Use of Sarum, a minor variant in non-essentials of the Roman rite, which had prevailed throughout Western Christendom in the late Middle Ages and had fallen into desuetude in the wake of the English Reformation. This had been his invariable practice in England, unless specifically prevented by clients in so doing, and was a logical component of his belief that: 'An Englishman needs not controversial writings to lead him to the faith of his fathers; it is written on the wall, on the window, on the pavement, by the highway.'[12] England would be led back to the 'ancient faith' most surely through the revival of those forms and rituals once intimately associated with it.

Having turned to European models for church buildings and furnishings early in his career, Pugin had been converted to a resolutely English path, in large part as a result of criticism from his friend Dr Daniel Rock, priest, antiquary and sometime chaplain to the Earl of Shrewsbury, who was the first to research and publish a detailed description and analysis of the Sarum Use. On the last page of *True Principles*, his most influential work, Pugin declared: 'I once stood on the very edge of a precipice in this respect, from which I was rescued by the advice and arguments of my respected and revered friend Dr Rock, to whose learned researches and observations on Christian antiquities I am highly indebted, and to whom I feel in bounden duty to make this public acknowledgement of the great benefit I have received from his advice.'[13] Building churches for a defunct liturgy was perhaps inevitable for a man who had learnt his religion from the

Fig 2.2 | One of Bishop Willson's forty silk Gothic chasubles, made in 1843 and remodelled in Roman form after 1934 [Tasmanian Museum and Art Gallery]

study of medieval antiquities, but there was an unbridgeable chasm between this viewpoint and Roman Catholic post-Reformation liturgical practice with its quite different requirements for church layout and furnishing. No wonder he had exclaimed in respect of his St Mary's Church, Dudley: 'The church at Dudley is a compleat [*sic*] facsimile of one of the old English parish churches, and nobody seems to know how to use it.'[14] And so it has remained.

A Sarum Use liturgy has never been celebrated in any of Pugin's churches. But for Willson at least, the intention to adopt the Use of Sarum was fully in accord with Pugin's position, and as such he was one of a tiny handful of like-minded Catholic clergy. His view of Tasmanian needs was co-extensive with English requirements, and this antipodean Colony was in many ways perceived as a distant County. On his first return visit to England in 1847 Willson purchased a rare Sarum Use missal, not as an antiquarian acquisition but to use for Mass in due course.[15] He would presumably celebrate this Mass using an equally rare late medieval English chalice and paten which he had acquired from Selim, Dean & Co of London on the same visit.[16]

The totality of Pugin and Willson's antipodean vision to meet the needs – literally from cradle to grave – of a flock comprising 3,000 convicts and 2,000 free Roman Catholics in scattered settlements and penal institutions across a wild and mountainous island was revealed in an address given by Willson to his clergy on 23 October 1844, some five months after his arrival in Van Diemen's Land:

> I ... procured not less than 40 sets of vestments – linen of every description for several churches – such as albs, surplices, amices, Altar cloths, Chalice linen etc. common cloths ... Crosses, Chalices, Ciboriums, Pixes [sic], holy oils stocks ... a portable Altar for use of the Bp when travelling – and in order to introduce the proper church style in this distant land, I also procured a font rightly constructed and fitted which will serve as a model for all other churches, also stone picinas [sic], stone crosses, models of churches constructed on proper scales all by the great restorer of Church architecture and church furniture Mr Pugin, together with a variety of things which I hope will tend & promote God's glory and your salvation.[17] [fig. 2.2]

He might also have mentioned one thousand works of piety and instruction, all with illustrations by Pugin and published by Thomas Richardson of Derby, who had become involved in such publishing through the efforts of Willson and Fr Thomas Sing of Derby. Two days before Willson's departure from England aboard the *Bella Marina* on 5 February 1844 *The Tablet* had noted with interest the cargo accompanying him:

> Vestments, albs, surplices, and all other articles of Church furniture are, we understand, on board, and a very extensive supply of prayer-books and books of instruction for the unfortunate prisoners who are the objects of the zeal and charity of this little band of missionaries; also models of churches of the most simple form, head-stones for graves,

and a variety of things that will be of use in carrying out the purposes of religion at the uttermost end of the earth ... May their voyage be pleasant and their mission prosperous.[18]

In addition to the exemplar font, Willson brought out a transitional Norman/ Early English baptismal font, which had doubtless been acquired by Pugin and then reconditioned by George Myers, including the fitting of a lid. Such an action in returning ecclesiastical antiquities to the purpose for which they had been made was an enduring characteristic of Pugin's work throughout his career, with numerous examples to be found in England and Ireland. This font would find a home in Willson's St Mary's Cathedral, Hobart, opened after his death.

Armed with first-hand experience of the situation in Tasmania and of the on-going needs of his diocese, Willson made further purchases from Hardmans and from George Myers during his 1847 return visit to England, greatly encouraged by Pugin who also made available much at no cost. Some items in their sheer numbers were remarkable, arising from the needs of a whole diocese as well as those of his clergy serving as Convict Department chaplains in penitentiaries and convict probation stations across the island. Thus, Myers' men carved at

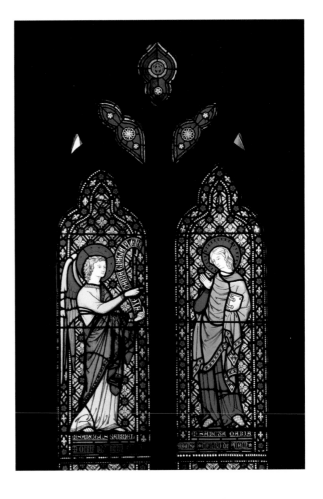

Fig 2.3 | The rood screen crucifix in St Patrick's Church, Colebrook, one of at least fourteen such Tasmanian figures by George Myers from a Pugin design of 1847 [Graham Lupp]

Fig 2.4 | A simple chalice designed by Pugin in 1847, one of a batch of ten destined for use in the convict service [Tasmanian Museum and Art Gallery]

Fig 2.5 | Pugin's 1847 gift window for Bishop Willson [Tasmanian Museum and Art Gallery]

least fourteen crucifix figures from White Pine, gessoed and polychromed them, all to the one Pugin design and of varying heights from 26 to 132cm. They were destined *inter alia* for rood screens and sacristies. [fig. 2.3] Their design was so late in Pugin's career that almost all examples are to be found in Tasmania, with just three others, all rood screen figures (two in England and one in Ireland) known elsewhere. Likewise, Pugin designed an elegantly simple chalice and paten for Willson, principally for use in the convict service, and Hardmans made ten sets for just £40, probably the largest single order for the one liturgical vessel in the firm's long career. [fig. 2.4] They were manufactured using contemporary methods such as steam presses and electro-deposition. Such practices were entirely consistent with remarks Pugin had made in 1843 regarding 'Modern Inventions and Mechanical Improvements' in respect of building construction when he stated: 'In matters purely mechanical, the Christian architect should gladly avail himself of those improvements and increased facilities that are suggested from time to time ... *It is only when mechanical invention intrudes on the confines of art, and tends to subvert the principles which it should advance, that it becomes objectionable*'.[19]

Pugin wrote to Hardman on 14 November 1847, while Willson was on a visit, urging him to do all possible to assist the Bishop's efforts:

> *Bishop Willson is here & is much delighted with all here. I am very anxious about his Diocese – he is so anxious to do all right – I have arranged for him to take out a quantity of casts – & also 2 or 3 tracery windows worked as patterns – 2 sorts of benches &c. Specimens of panelling, in fact models by which he will be able to produce work on the spot. It has occurred to me that Early must have a great quantity of stencils & if we were to transfer the patterns on sheets of paper they would be exceedingly useful – so pray see to this. Give to him 1st stencils of various patterns 2. Rubbings of our brasses which they could imitate in incised stones [Then follow items to be sold to Willson] The Bishop tells me he got our plain Candlesticks cast in Hobart Town. Could he not do the same with our plain processional cross. Pray think if there is anything else we could help him with. It appears to me one of the most important things to accomplish to introduce the true form of sacred things in the new world. Rely on it as it begins it must go on for having so few models people will naturally follow what they see. I am going to give him all the drawings unused cartoons &c. that I can. I am getting 12 sorts of headstones for him. I want Mrs. Powell to have a set of silk & gold apparels of any colour got ready for him ... I am very anxious to establish a regular correspondence with Bishop Willson – so as to keep him supplied with such things as he may require.*[20]

All in all, Pugin supplied Willson with sixteen exemplar headstones, and these were replicated in sandstone with varying degrees of competence by Tasmanian stonemasons right up to the end of the nineteenth century. Well over sixty Pugin-designed headstones are to be found in Roman Catholic graveyards, from Campbell Town in the north to Franklin in the south, not to mention large numbers of local variants of the original designs.

Willson's 1847 visit yielded other examples both of a strong friendship and of an alignment of ideals with Pugin. Writing to Hardman on 16 November 1847, Pugin again touched on the subject of items for Willson: 'I did not mean you to send the *actual* stencils to Dr Willson but to stencil the patterns on *sheets of paper* & give him one real stencil as a guide – I have a great mind to give him the annunciation in glass we were going to send to Barn town & make another – but even in that case I should have the *heads* repainted. What do you say to that?'[21] Two days later he communicated his decision to Hardman: 'I will give him the glass – so repaint the heads – it will be considered a treasure over there.'[22] George Myers' men carved the stone tracery which accompanied the glass to Hobart. The window, installed in Willson's then pro-cathedral of St Joseph, bears a unique testimony to the close and enduring friendship between the two men. Across the base is the supplication, '*Orate pro bono statu Augusti Welby de Pugin*' (Pray for the good estate of Augustus Welby de Pugin). [fig. 2.5]

In May of 1847 Pugin and Willson were both in Rome and had separate audiences with Pope Pius IX. Willson was presented with the customary chalice in the neo-Classical idiom of the period, whose subsequent fate speaks volumes for the two friends' shared principles and abhorrence of Pagan intrusions. The chalice was sent to Hardmans, melted down, extra silver added and re-made to a new Pugin design.[23] Under the base was engraved: '+ Gift of his Holiness Pius the IXth to Robert William + Bishop of Hobart Town + Rome + May + Mdcccxlvii'. Well, most of the silver was! Willson paid Hardmans just £6–18–0 for another chalice in 1847, being for the fitting of a new bowl to a fourteenth-century Sienese chalice supplied by Pugin. This was one of at least five examples of Pugin recycling Sienese chalices, arising from the same motive as for Willson's medieval font. In Tasmania such objects would underscore the legitimate continuity of the tiny, impoverished Catholic underclass with the ancient faith of England.

It was not until 1850 that Willson could see his way clear financially to construct the first church from one of Pugin's models. It was not just the poverty of his flock, over half of whom as aforementioned were convicts. He had also inherited a large unanticipated debt arising from the construction of St Joseph's, Hobart, by Fr John Joseph Therry, despite assurances having been given by Archbishop Polding at the time of the Hobart appointment that such would not be the case. On 9 April he laid the foundation stone of the little two-compartment church of St Paul at Oatlands in the Southern Midlands. Writing to his episcopal friend Bishop Goold of Melbourne a few days later he remarked, 'I had the consolation to lay the first stone of a little church at Oatlands – mine will be a very humble building, still it will afford the means of accommodation to a flock for divine worship.'[24] Plans had been prepared from the model by Frederick Hugh Thomas (1817–1885), who 'moonlighted' for Willson whilst in the employ of the Public Works Department as an architectural draughtsman. Thomas had been sentenced to Transportation for forgery, so would have been ideally suited, one would imagine, to making accurate copies.

St Paul's Church, opened on 28 February 1851, was a scholarly evocation of a small English medieval village church, conceding nothing to its Australian setting. [fig. 2.6] The vocabulary of its elements established that it reflected progressive construction that would have taken place between around 1200 and 1320. In its plan form, composition and furnishings it conformed to Pugin's exposition of what constituted 'a complete Catholic parish church for the due celebration of the divine office and administration of the sacraments, both as regards architectural arrangement and furniture', as set out in his 1841 *Dublin Review* article 'On the Present State of Ecclesiastical Architecture in England'.[25] It comprised an aisled four-bay nave with south porch, a relatively deep separately-expressed chancel, with a rood screen across the chancel arch, and a sacristy in the angle between the nave east wall and the chancel north wall. Notable was the absence of an external door to the sacristy, something to be found in all Pugin's churches except those in Tasmania. This was likely the result of Fr Ullathorne's view

Fig 2.6 | St Paul's Church, Oatlands (1850–51), photographed in the 1860s
[Archdiocese of Hobart Archives]

of Tasmania as being vulnerable to the misdeeds of convicts and bushrangers. There was a west door for ceremonial usage, such as processions or the visit of a bishop, and the chancel was fitted with sedilia and a piscina in the south wall, an Easter sepulchre – a simple niche – in the north wall opposite the sedilia and standard candlesticks. It was thus liturgically furnished for the Use of Sarum. Lancet windows typical of the Early English period lit the nave north and south walls. The chancel east window was a three-light Flowing Decorated design with reticulated tracery, a type much admired and very widely used in churches built around 1320. It was the most elaborately developed element in the building's structure, and that for reasons of propriety.

In *True Principles* Pugin had defined propriety as an essential attribute of a building, whereby '*the external and internal appearance of an edifice should be illustrative of, and in accordance with, the purpose for which it is destined*'.[26] For churches, this meant that the chancel should be the most highly elaborated part of the building because it was, in Pugin's view, 'the most sacred part of the edifice'. The sedilia in St Paul's were simple in form, and designed to be made from

Fig 2.7 | St Patrick's Church, Colebrook (1855–57)
[Brian Andrews]

wood as for the two other model churches. The piscina, to the east of the sedilia, was copied from one of the two stone exemplar piscinas carved by George Myers' men and brought out with the church models by Bishop Willson, as were the holy water stoups. A churchyard cross, likewise copied from a stone exemplar, stood in the churchyard. The wooden furnishings were constructed from Australian cedar (*Toona Australis*) by Patrick John Lynch (1804–1889) who had arrived in Tasmania as an assisted migrant from Ireland in 1854. Lynch was a skilled cabinetmaker who had been engaged on Pugin's and John Gregory Crace's decorative program at Lismore Castle, County Waterford, for the Duke of Devonshire. The only exception was the rood screen crucifix, which was one of the Pugin-designed figures brought back to Hobart by Willson in 1847. The altar was designed by Willson's architect protégé Henry Hunter (1832–1892) after an 1854 Hardman altar supplied for St Joseph's, Hobart. Hunter painted and gilded the altar and reredos himself, the decoration being copied from Pugin's *Glossary*, and it was complete with riddel curtains.[27] Although the Anglican clergyman Frederick Holdship Cox had built an ecclesiologically correct church, St John the

Baptist's, Prosser's Plains, Tasmania, between 1846 and 1849 (based on Richard Cromwell Carpenter's St John the Baptist's, Cookham Dean), it possessed not one of the furnishings proper to the Use of Sarum. It was left to St Paul's to be the first comprehensive antipodean realisation of the Pugin ideal.

Pugin's second church model was copied for the construction of St Patrick's, Colebrook, commenced in 1855 and opened on 21 January 1857. An extreme example of Pugin's approach to the design of a small inexpensive church, it was compositionally unique in his *oeuvre*, being an aisled, clerestoried building in the Decorated style, with a three-bay nave, a rood screen with Pugin crucifix figure, a relatively deep separately-expressed chancel, an antipodean north porch and a large triple bellcote astride the nave east gable. A sacristy without an exterior door abutted the south aisle east wall and the chancel south wall. [fig. 2.7] Possibly intended as a town church, it finished up being erected on the outskirts of the burgeoning settlement of Jerusalem – now Colebrook – thirty kilometres south of Oatlands. Again, Frederick Thomas produced the drawings and supervised the work, while Patrick Lynch was both the builder and the maker of the Australian cedar furnishings. Carved in a moulded blind triangle on the west gable was the date of commencement, the lettering copied from one of Willson's two stone exemplar Pugin alphabets from 1843.

Pugin's imperative to provide Willson with 'simple buildings that can be easily erected' was dramatically realised here in both composition and detail. St Patrick's would be the most astringent, pared-back church he was ever to create, relying for the harmony of its interior on superb composition combined with pure line and form, a text-book essay on his 'True Principles'. On the continuum of Pugin's churches in terms of structural and decorative elaboration, St Giles, Cheadle, regarded by some as England's finest nineteenth-century parish church, occupies one extreme and St Patrick's, Colebrook, the other. Undoubtedly the most radical aspect of the minimal interior was the nave arcade. [fig. 2.8] This consisted of square columns with neither capitals nor bases, the plain chamfer to their corners continuing up as the moulding to the arches. The chamfers ended in a pyramidal stop 61cm from the floor. Like Oatlands, details such as the gable crosses, the holy water stoup and the piscina were copied from exemplar stonework, as was the churchyard cross standing in the adjacent cemetery.

St Patrick's Church was opened on 21 January 1857. Its beauty captivated the correspondent who covered the event for the *Tasmanian Daily News*. These were sentiments already expressed by the church's first pastor, Fr William Dunne, who had written to a priestly colleague during its construction, declaring, 'it will be the most beautiful church in the Island, and cost over £1,500 cash. The style is Gothic – real Middle Age – and the site is admirably chosen.'[28]

By 1858, Goodridge's 'Gothick' church of St John's, Richmond, must have seemed decidedly unfashionable to Fr Dunne, having just erected St Patrick's, Colebrook. The as-yet unused third model presented a potentially useful source of components to convert the existing building into one that was more

Fig 2.8 | The interior of St Patrick's Church, Colebrook (1855–57) [Brian Andrews]

ecclesiologically appropriate, with a chancel, sacristy, tower and spire. The problem in using Pugin's third model design for the extensions was that it was for a church substantially larger than St John's. Frederick Thomas was charged with adapting parts of the model. That Thomas was no Pugin is evident from the results. Goodridge's church, with new diagonal buttressing to the corners, was retained as the nave. Thomas tacked on a single-bay chancel which was a reduced-scale version of that on the model. The ungainly trussed rafter roof for the chancel, with collar ties just above the wall plate level, was almost certainly a Thomas touch, as was the awkward four-centred chancel arch. Fitting a reduced-size rood screen, extracted from the model, across the chancel arch proved beyond Thomas's competence and he substituted conventional communion rails. He did, however, install sedilia and a piscina in the chancel south wall and added a scaled-down version of the model sacristy against the chancel north wall. The tower and spire presented an even greater challenge. Thomas crudely solved the problem of the disparity in size by simply guillotining the belfry stage and shortening the lowest one, but in his ignorance left the spire at its original size. The result was comical to say the least, with a massive spire perched like a dunce's cap on the squat vestigial tower, whose lowest buttress set-offs were virtually at ground level. He inserted one of the two-light plate tracery lights from the omitted belfry stage into the west face of the tower upper stage.

Willson's espousal of Pugin's vision for the antipodes resulted in a splendid heritage of metalwork, textiles, carved wood and stonework and much more across Tasmania. And the three little village churches, with their churchyard crosses and headstones, all within a distance of less than 60km 'at the uttermost end of the earth', speak perhaps as nowhere else of that flawed vision for a Roman Catholic landscape:

> *Every true son of the revival will utterly reject the miserable support of those who would limit its restoration to certain degrees of latitude or boundaries of provinces. No; wherever the Cross of Christ is planted and His faith preached, there ought the cruciform church arise – there ought the mystery of the Holy Trinity be symbolised by triple window and triequal division, and pillar and pinnacle and cross-crowned spires rise towards Heaven, the sign of the resurrection of the body and life everlasting.*[29]

NOTES

1. Pugin to Hardman, 16 November 1847, in Margaret Belcher (ed.), *The Collected Letters of A.W.N. Pugin*, vol. 3, Oxford, 2009, p.313. Excerpts from Pugin's letters have been quoted with corrected spelling.

2. 'Catholic Intelligence. Catholic church architecture. Letter of A.W.N. Pugin, Esq.', *The Tablet*, vol. 9 (2 September 1848), p. 563.

3. Willson to Goold, 13 March 1851, Archdiocese of Hobart Archives (hereafter AHA), Willson Papers, CA.6/WIL.465.

4. Cited in W.T. Southerwood, *The Convict's Friend: A Life of Bishop Robert William Willson*, George Town, 1989, p.1.

5. Willson to Fitzpatrick, Shrove Tuesday [1859], Melbourne Diocesan Historical Commission.

6. Brian Andrews, *Creating a Gothic Paradise: Pugin at the Antipodes*, Hobart, 2002, p.54. This exhibition catalogue is the fullest exposition to date of Pugin's Tasmanian works.

7. Leo Madigan (ed.), *The Devil is a Jackass*, Leominster, 1995, pp.67–8.

8. A.W.N Pugin, *Contrasts*, London, 2nd edn, 1841, p.14.

9. Pugin to Shrewsbury, 30 January 1844, in Belcher, *Collected Letters*, vol. 2 (2003), p.161.

10. Pugin to Bloxam, 26 August 1843, *ibid.*, p.101.

11. Andrews, *op. cit.* [note 6], p.72.

12. A.W.N Pugin, *An Apology for the Revival of Christian Architecture in England*, London, 1843, p.49.

13. A.W.N Pugin, *The True Principles of Pointed or Christian Architecture*, London, 1841, p.76.

14. Pugin to Ambrose Lisle Phillipps, 18 December 1840, in Belcher, *Collected Letters*, vol. 1 (2001), p.175.

15. The missal was printed in 1527 by Christoffel van Ruremond in Antwerp and published in London by Franz Birkman.

16. The chalice dates from *c*.1470–80 and the paten has been dated after 1450. See Charles Oman, *English Church Plate 597–1830*, London, 1957, p.305.

17. Draft of a speech by Bishop Willson on 'the state of church temporalities', given to a meeting of the clergy and others, Hobart, 23 October 1844, AHA, Willson Papers, CA.6/WIL.12.

18. *The Tablet*, vol. 5:195 (3 February 1844), p.69.

19. Pugin, *op. cit.* [note 12], pp.39–40.

20. Pugin to Hardman, 14 November 1847, Belcher, *op. cit.* [note 1], pp.310–11. Thomas Earley (1819–1893), habitually misspelt 'Early' by Pugin, was a Hardman employee who executed much of Pugin's painted flat decorative work.

21. Pugin to Hardman, 16 November 1847, Belcher, *op. cit.* [note 1], p.314.

22. Pugin to Hardman, 18 November 1847, *ibid.*, p.315.

23. Birmingham City Archives, Hardman Archive, Metal Day Book, 2 December 1847, p.258: 'Rt Revd Bishop Willson Hobart Town A Silver Chalice & Paten, remade & Silver added, &c. with legend 'Gift of His Holiness Pius the IX to Robert William, Bishop of Hobart Town' 8 0 0'.

24. Willson to Goold, St Mark's day [25 April] 1850, AHA, Willson Papers, CA.6/WIL/465.

25. [A.W.N Pugin] 'On the Present State of Ecclesiastical Architecture in England', *Dublin Review*, vol. 10 (May 1841), pp.312–48.

26. Pugin, *op.cit.* [note 13], p.50.

27. Hunter was propelled into an architectural career by Bishop Willson in 1855 in the aftermath of Pugin's death in 1852. He went on to become Tasmania's most prolific nineteenth-century architect, designing more than forty Anglican and Catholic churches in a Puginesque idiom. See Andrews, *op.cit.* [note 6], pp.142–59.

28. Dunne to McEncroe, *c*.1855, quoted in John H. Cullen, 'Bishop Willson', *Australasian Catholic Record*, vol. 30:1 (January 1953), p.43.

29. *Op. cit.* [note 2].

3 · The Ecclesiology of Expediency in Colonial Australia

MILES LEWIS

The greatest test of any culture arises when it is moved out of its traditional comfort zone. It may have to survive under political restrictions, active suppression or even persecution. It may involve traditional practices which are irrelevant, impractical or offensive to the society in which it now finds itself. It may require artefacts, buildings or items of food which can no longer be readily obtained. To meet such challenges it may have to surrender or compromise is tenets: but alternatively it may find an acceptable way to adapt to the new constraints.

All these things happened in the nineteenth century to church building practices in locations distant from Europe – that is, removed from their traditional base: from sources of ecclesiastical authority, design guidance, traditional building materials, skilled builders and artisans. Conditions in the Australian colonies, and in comparable new world settlements generally, severely constrained church building. Massy stone buildings in the Gothic style, with ornate carving and rich stained glass were generally not feasible.

The climate was often unsuitable for churches designed along established ecclesiological lines; settlements were often transient, so that it made little sense to invest in substantial church buildings; money was often extremely limited; local building materials were untried, unconventional or ephemeral; skilled labour was usually very scarce and/or enormously expensive; and the climate might call for lightweight construction, cross-ventilation, and broad eaves for sun protection.

This did not mean that ecclesiological principles were thrown to the winds. There were serious efforts to make light timber frames conform to English medieval traditions, and to make prefabricated iron buildings look other than purely industrial. But most of these efforts are best characterised as shifts and expedients – simplified architectural styles, framed tent churches, corrugated iron combined with pointed windows; timber frames stained to look like oak, stained glass replicated in oiled fabric; and plate iron church fronts concealing corrugated iron carcases.

Those who designed the first churches in New South Wales were amateurs, and had in any case left England at a time when churches were hardly being built. The *Church Building Act* was a thing of the future, and the Camden Society more distant still. Georgian churches were often more classical than medieval in style. The early churches of Sydney were naive designs and primitive constructions,

Detail of fig 3.9 | Interior view of the second church erected for the Diocese of Melbourne at Hemming's Patent Improved Portable Buildings Manufactory, Bristol [State Library of Victoria].

Fig 3.1 | Holy Trinity Church Kelso (near Bathurst), New South Wales (1833–5).
Tower added later [Ian Sutton, Wikipedia Commons].

but in other respects were not really out of the British mainstream. St Phillip's
was castellated in a medieval way, but the dressed arched window openings had
more to do with the Renaissance: there was certainly no pretence to any sort of
stylistic accuracy. Scots Church, a little later and probably designed by Dr John
Dunmore Lang, was more recognisably Gothic, but with intersecting tracery at
the entrance reminiscent of Georgian and Regency shop windows, and double
lancet windows owing most to the 'Gothick' tradition exemplified by William
Kent in the early eighteenth century.[1]

But Holy Trinity, Kelso (which survives today), seems a genuine throwback [fig.
3.1]. By the 1830s things had moved on in England: hundreds of Commissioners'
churches had been built, antiquarian researches had progressed, and the first
stirrings of the Gothic Revival were occurring. And more importantly, quite sophisticated churches were beginning to appear in the Australian colonies.

The first real indication of a conscious response to the constraints upon
church building in the colonies comes in the work of James Blackburn (1803–
1854) in Van Diemen's Land, now Tasmania. Blackburn was a convict, and nothing is known of any architectural training that he may have had. His work makes
extensive use of Loudon's *Encyclopædia*,[2] contrary to the impressions of Lady

Fig 3.2 | Presbyterian Church, Sorell, by Jams Blackburn,
designed 1839 [Miles Lewis].

Jane Franklin, wife of the Governor of Van Diemen's Land, who wrote in 1839: 'It appears that there is not a single book, on architecture in all the island except my own Loudon's Farm and Cottage Architecture.' And his work draws upon other sources as well, as in his Presbyterian Church at Sorrell (1839 onwards) [fig. 3.2].[3]

It is at first difficult to see how Blackburn would have developed an interest in the Norman style. The Norman was a fashion just emerging in England, but it reached its height in the 1840s,[4] too late to have influenced Blackburn, and he seems unlikely to have known Daniel Robertson's St Clement's, Oxford (1827–8).[5] Likewise, the 'laughable' Romanesque churches by John Cunningham of Liverpool were begun in 1837,[6] and the North Italian Romanesque churches of J.W. Wild and Wyatt & Brandon date from after 1840.[7] However, there is a fairly close precedent in a pattern book by G.E. Hamilton, *Designs for Rural Churches* (1836). Blackburn's square axial tower, the corner turret, and the panel of blind arcading on the tower all occur in Hamilton's design.

We can also get some idea of why Norman might have been thought a suitable style for churches in Tasmania. As Ian Lochhead points out in the current volume, two years later, in 1841, the Norman style was chosen for churches in New Zealand. The rationale for this was explained in words which are generally taken to be those of Bishop Selwyn (but are more likely those of Beresford Hope or of the Ecclesiological Society's architect, Anthony Salvin, who was to produce the required design, and had already been consulted at this stage):

> Norman is the style adopted; because, as the work will be chiefly done by native artists, it seems natural to teach them first that style which first prevailed in our own country; while its rudeness and massiveness, and the grotesque character of its sculpture, will probably render it easier to be understood and appreciated by them.[8]

The design produced by Salvin for the Cambridge Camden Society was not the English Norman style of Hamiltion and Blackburn, but was instead based upon that of St-Étienne at Thaon (Than) near Caen in Normandy.[9] However, the reasoning was probably similar: conditions in Tasmania were seen as being similarly primitive, and the rudeness and massiveness as being appropriate to convict artisans as much as to Maoris. In detailing the church at Sorell is indeed crude, and probably nothing like what Hamilton would have recommended. But some of the details do clearly derive from Hamilton.

In the remoter areas of the Australian colonies one might expect to find *ad hoc* churches of materials such as wattle and daub, sods, adobe, and bark, but in fact these are surprisingly rare. What one finds instead are frames and tents of various types, especially on the goldfields. And often they were built ostensibly as schools, so as to be eligible for a government subsidy, but intended also for use as churches on Sunday.

The framed tent is an almost forgotten building type, and requires a little explanation. It was a timber frame, like the frame of a cottage, covered in a canvas envelope, made up by a tentmaker or sailmaker. The reason why these buildings are largely forgotten is that they gradually turned into conventional buildings. When the earth floor got too dusty it was boarded. When the roof got too leaky it was clad in shingles or corrugated iron. When the sides got too rotten, or burglars cut through the canvas, they were clad in weatherboard. When the building proved too cold it was given a fireplace and a wall lining. And it had now become a conventional wooden building, almost indistinguishable from the normal type.

The practice of dual use continued past the goldfield tent stage into conventional buildings. It led to the designs which were officially schools, but looked remarkably like churches, and sometimes the chancel was partitioned off to prevent it being used on weekdays by the school.

By the late 1840s there were many Englishmen in Australia who had been influenced by the Ecclesiological movement. W.A. Sandford, Colonial Secretary of Western Australia, was a member of the Cambridge Camden (later Ecclesiological) Society, and this is reflected in his design for a boys school.[10] More important were bishops such as W.G. Broughton of New South Wales, and G.A. Selwyn of New Zealand.[11]

The use of exposed framing as a picturesque device was well established in England by the early nineteenth century, and by no means confined to the

Ecclesiologists or to church architecture generally. It was particularly promoted by S.H. Brooks in his *Cottage and Villa Architecture* of about 1839, with designs in a variety of styles, and generally with brick or other solid nogging between the framing.[12] This domestic use of exposed framing had an impact in New Zealand, from where Bishop Selwyn's chaplain, William Cotton, wrote in 1843 to his sister Phoebe, asking her to visit cottages recently built at Rooknest in Surrey and to sketch the best of them, 'as I think it very likely we may be able to build in the same style which shows the timber, in all manner of odd shapes between the plaster panels.'[13] In Australia the exposed timber frame is generally seen as being a special characteristic of Queensland vernacular architecture, but its real impact was in churches.

Although medieval English churches are overwhelmingly of stone – at least the surviving ones – a few, such as SS James and Paul, Marton, Cheshire, founded in 1843, and the fourteenth-century nave of St Peter, Besford, Worcestershire, are timber-framed. Architects trying to find suitable designs for the colonies, especially in the tropics, seized upon these as a precedent. The Ecclesiologists thought the exposed frame appropriate for timber churches, especially in tropical and other colonial areas. R.C. Carpenter's design for a wooden church for Tristan da Cunha[14] is well-known, but it comes well after developments in New Zealand and Australia. There were a number of other examples too.[15]

St Mark's Church at Picton, Western Australia (1841), though it is a primitive structure of wattle and daub with a thatched roof, is self-consciously Gothic. Indeed, the Rev. J.B. Wollaston used 'calico prepared with oil and turpentine and painted with cross-stripes in imitation of Quarries' for the windows.[16] An even clearer example was Christ Church, Kiama, New South Wales (1843), probably designed by Bishop Broughton himself the previous year, when he was visited by Bishop Selwyn of New Zealand.[17] Selwyn himself would later adopt a half-timbered style Gothic architecture for his own chapel at St John's College, Auckland, with the assistance of the architect-cum-priest, Frederick Thatcher (see Lochhead article in current volume). One very beautiful example of the type survives in Victoria. Christ Church, Tarraville, was designed in 1855 by the local architect J.H.W. Pettit (of Pettit & Hastings), and is quite sophisticated, with ornamental chamfer-stopped framing members and an infill of horizontal sawn planks joined with quarter inch splines [fig. 3.3].[18] Few other such churches survive except in Queensland, where the technique was introduced in the late 1860s for both churches and schools by the architect Richard Suter, who had connections with both Cambridge and New Zealand.[19]

The first exposed frame building in Queensland is cited as the Methodist church at Bundamba, said, but not reliably so, to date from 1865, though it has not been proved to be Suter's work.[20] However, the first school with exposed framing was built at Nanango in 1865–6, almost certainly to Suter's design, and probably while he was working in the office of Benjamin Backhouse.[21] The building is unusual in that the lining boards were placed vertically, but they were diagonal

Fig 3.3 | Christ Church, Tarraville, Victoria, by J. H. W.
Pettit of Pettit & Hastings, 1855–6 [Alex Bremner]

in the church at Lutwyche, and also in the school at Oxley Creek (1866), the first
which can be definitely attributed to Suter.[22] Others of his schools, like that at
Beenleigh, had the horizontal boarding which was to become the Queensland
norm [fig. 3.4].

Exposed frame churches and schools were soon built by other architects in
Queensland, and some were built elsewhere in Australia, such as the Presbyterian
Church at Tenterfield, New South Wales, where what was exposed was simply
a utilitarian stud frame without ornamental development.[23] Most importantly,
the technique spread from churches and schools to houses and other buildings,
in which it has become familiar as a characteristic Queensland vernacular form.

Prefabrication is another tradition of great age, but its modern history begins
in the 1830s and 1840s, when 'portable' houses were sent from Britain to Africa,
India and California, a flour mill to Turkey, lighthouses to Ceylon and Bermuda,
and churches to Trinidad and South Australia. Prefabrication is always more expensive than conventional building, but it becomes worthwhile in circumstances
where an impermanent site location or new settlement has been chosen; where
differential labour costs between the source and site occur; when a lack of materials is apparent; or when economies of scale in production are difficult. The
first three of these factors were often important in the construction of colonial

Fig 3.4 | St Patrick's Roman Catholic Church, Ravenswood, 1871
(east end 1905–6) [Miles Lewis].

churches, though the fourth was barely relevant. In fact, in many Australian coastal settlements the bulk of building was done in imported timber until the mid-nineteenth century, so there was every reason to do the work at the point of origin if labour was cheaper there.

Peter Thompson, of Commercial Road, Limehouse, London, was a prominent manufacturer of prefabricated buildings, which he supplied to Adelaide and elsewhere.[24] He was also a pioneer of concrete, and of terra cotta block construction: his church at Reigate in 1853 was made of blocks, which were noted for presenting a good face on both sides.[25] Thompson appears to have begun as a prefabricator to supply the English domestic market, many noblemen and gentlemen having been induced, he claimed, 'to have Ornamental Cottages, Shooting Boxes, and Villas built in this manner, in England'.[26] By 1839 at least he was advertising houses for export to South Australia in Stephens's *The Land of Promise*.[27] In 1841 he advertised in the *Colonial Magazine* that his houses were suitable for all the British colonies,[28] and in 1843 he was reported to have sent a two-storey house of twelve rooms to Madras.[29]

In 1844 Thompson sent an iron church to Jamaica.[30] At some time in the 1840s he received a treasury grant permitting him to manufacture and export free of duty framed churches, chapels, schools and dwellings for 'her Majesty's various colonies'.[31] The Adelaide church was brought out by the Colonial Chaplain, C.B. Howard, at the end of 1836,[32] together with a house by Henry Manning. The two buildings were obtained simultaneously by the Church Society, which had received subscriptions of over £800, more than half of this amount being from the Society for the Promotion of Christian Knowledge.[33] The church was described as being 'a frame one':[34] a handsome structure for 750 persons, which took up the whole cargo space of the *William Hutt*. However, it was found by Colonel Light to be too flimsy to be used,[35] and the materials were adapted for use in building the first schoolroom.[36] In fact, according to the *Register*, the only part of the church then existing was 'a strange wooden extinguisher ... the steeple'. The other components were either not supplied, did not fit, were splintered, or rotten.[37]

Wooden churches were not a major item of export to Australia, nor to the other colonies. But there was a range of other materials, including Smallwood's 'portable brick' system, which in fact consisted of tile hung on a timber frame, not unlike traditional mathematical tiling. As reported in August 1853:

> the building is formed of timber, and covered outside with a face of tiles, which give it the aspect of a brick building. The timber is metal tongued, and is so cut and arranged as to be usable for packing goods on the voyage, and readily erected afterwards. The patentee is Mr Smallwood, of Camden-Town, the inventor of the Convex and Concave Hollow Tiles.[38]

According to Smallwood's advertisement, the timber was metal-tongued yellow deal wainscoting. The system was said to be adapted to houses, chapels, bazaars, galleries and stores, the cost of a chapel to seat five hundred being £375.[39]

The most surprising of all prefabrication systems was that using papier mâché [fig. 3.5a-b]. C. F. Bielefeld was originally an ordinary papier mâché manufacturer, of trays, knick knacks, etc., and he began to specialise in architectural components like cornices and centre flowers for ceilings. Then he made partitions for steamship cabins, and finally developed waterproof papier mâché and a system for complete buildings. The church illustrated here formed part of a complete village which was to be taken to Australia by a Mr Seymour. It seems that the buildings arrived, but were not put up in a single village, for there are odd references to 'paper houses' in Melbourne and Geelong rate books. But the fate of the church is unknown.

Iron churches on the other hand are numerous, both in the Australian colonies and elsewhere. Peter Thompson's iron church for Jamaica has been mentioned. Thomas Edington and Son's church 'for the Continent' in 1846,[40] an iron church and chapel made in Belgium in 1849 (for the Missionary Society of Brussels),[41] and an iron church designed for Rangoon by Matthew Digby Wyatt,[42] can probably all be accepted as true prefabricated iron buildings. But some are very unusual. A former Presbyterian church was put up at Numbaa, New South Wales, in 1854, together with two cognate structures, a hotel and a house [fig. 3.6]. It apparently had an attached porch, which might have made it seem slightly more ecclesiastical.

The church was made by Edwin Maw of Liverpool. Maw is first heard of in 1850,

Figs 3.5 a & b | Papier mâché
church [C. F. Bielefeld, *Portable
Buildings*, London 1853].

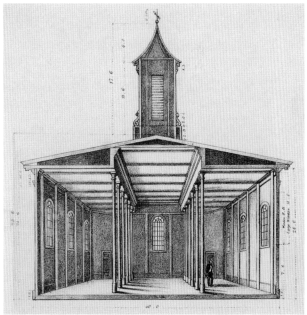

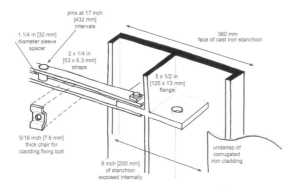

pins at 17 inch
[432 mm]
intervals

1.1/4 in [32 mm]
diameter sleeve
spacer

2 x 1/4 in
[53 x 6.3 mm]
straps

360 mm
face of cast iron stanchion

5 x 1/2 in
[125 x 13 mm]
flange

5/16 inch [7.6 mm]
thick chair for
cladding fixing bolt

underlap of
corrugated
iron cladding

8 inch [200 mm]
of stanchion
exposed internally

Fig 3.6 | Presbyterian church, Numbaa, New South Wales, 1854 [Miles Lewis].

Fig 3.7 | Edwin Maw's system of prefabricated iron construction, as seen at Longford House, Tasmania [Miles Lewis].

Fig 3.8 | Free Presbyterian church for Sydney (later St Stephen's church), photo of 1871 [New South Wales Government Printer].

when he sent iron buildings to California,[43] but his main business seems to have been the manufacture of railway rolling stock and equipment. He had a foundry at Liverpool on the north side of the Wallasey Pool, Seacombe, and early in 1851 he had let out four acres to one Godwin for a pottery works,[44] and it seems clear that Maw himself was some relation of J.H. Maw, the prominent manufacturer of encaustic tiles. By 1854 he found himself in financial difficulties, and on 8 June assigned his personal estate to Thomas Truss, 'overlooker of the rolling stock of the Shrewsbury and Chester Railway', probably one of his major customers.[45]

Although the church at Numbaa is shed-like and totally unecclesiastical, it is distinguished by the use of iron Polonceau roof trusses in four panels, with ornamental bifurcated cast iron struts. However, the top chord of the truss, like the girts, consists of two parallel bars spaced apart with short cylindrical pins, not unlike a bicycle chain. This is not a very rational form for a compression member, and the trusses have in fact failed to varying degrees. The corrugated iron cladding is carried on horizontal girts of a similar character, which is a marginally less absurd application of them. I have been able to reconstruct the system from another Edwin Maw building which survives in Tasmania, an outbuilding of 'Longford House' at Longford [fig. 3.7]. I surmise that these chain-like girts were something which Maw already used in his rolling stock business. An attractive hypothesis is that they were used for the sides of rail wagons and might have cladding attached to them or not, as required.

The most impressive of all the iron churches were produced in Glasgow, and were quite different from iron buildings made in England. Glasgow benefitted

especially from the Australian gold rushes, and a periodical solely devoted to the Australian trade, *McPhun's Australian News,* was published in 1853–4. A pair of iron churches was ordered by the Free Presbyterians for Melbourne and Sydney from Robertson & Lister of Glasgow [fig. 3.8]. They are elaborately fronted in cast plate iron, looking at first sight like conventional masonry buildings, but the sides are of heavy gauge corrugated iron. Three or four Glasgow firms specialised in these plate iron structures.

Complete corrugated iron buildings were far more common in Australia, and most of these were made in England. Some, like Holy Trinity (as it was to become), at Bacchus Marsh, Victoria, are anonymous. It was opened in July 1855, measured 46ft. 6in. by 28ft., and could accommodate between 150 and 200 people. It had vertical corrugated iron cladding without any vertical dividing members, pointed windows apparently in timber frames, and a tower clad in horizontal corrugated iron continuing across blind pointed windows in the base. The spire was square, flaring out at the base, and also clad in horizontal iron.[46] Others can be attributed to one or other of about four British manufacturers. The most prominent manufacturer of all was Samuel Hemming, of the Clift House Works at Bedminster, Bristol, and later of London. He began by making a house for a son who was going to Australia, and entered the business only at the time of the Victorian gold rush (1851). At these works a complete village was said to rise and fall each week as the buildings (houses, shops and churches) were constructed, labelled, dismantled, packed and despatched.

When Bishop Charles Perry planned to import churches to Melbourne he was fortunate in obtaining the approval of the Society for Promoting Christian Knowledge, which made a grant to assist the project.[47] Perry then approached the Birmingham manufacturer J.H. Porter, who quoted £3 a seat as his minimum price, but Hemming halved this by offering a church for six hundred at £1,000, for eight hundred at £1,250, and for one thousand at £1,500; greater sizes than this were not recommended. The freight was to cost about £200 and the iron parsonages £200 complete (though a later reference gives the same church prices as inclusive of freight, but the cost of a six room parsonage with flooring as £345).[48] 'We may soon be gratified,' according to an English report which was quoted in the *Church of England Messenger* in 1853, 'with the novel spectacle of clergymen leaving our shores from time to time for Port Phillip, each of these taking his church and parsonage house with him.'[49] This was exactly the procedure followed in one or two instances, though not by the Anglicans.

The construction of the churches was to be a wooden framework with the sides covered with 'plates' of galvanized iron and the interior lined with thin boards with an air space of about 3.9in. to be filled with an insulating material such as wool, straw, sawdust or sun-dried bricks [fig. 3.9]. The boarding was to be covered first with canvas and then with 'paper of a neat pattern'. The design was said to be pleasing in appearance, with a small belfry and tower in front. The nave had two aisles, and the pulpit, divisions of pews and other fittings, were of 'light and open ironwork'. The parsonage consisted of six ground floor rooms and had a 'pretty villa like appearance, with a deep verandah, and venetian blinds to exclude the heat.'[50]

The first of the churches was assembled at Bristol before shipment, and a service was held in it by the Venerable T. Hart Davies, late Archdeacon of Melbourne, assisted by the Rev. Dr Spencer and the Rev. H.G. Eland: the choristers of Bedminster attended and a collection of £57 was taken up.[51] This church was destined, with a parsonage, for Williamstown (now a bayside suburb of Melbourne)[52] where the need for church accommodation had been aggravated by the number of ships in the bay and, as it was reported in 1854,

> The difficulty of procuring workmen renders it impossible to erect a stone building; and a wooden church is objectionable for its instability and expense. To meet this exigency, however, the Bishop of Melbourne having ascertained the suitableness of iron buildings, as they are at present made, for this climate, has written home to procure iron for the purpose of iron churches and parsonage houses. It was therefore resolved ... that steps be taken immediately to secure an iron church and parsonage for Williamstown ... [53]

The church was mistakenly consigned to Melbourne, incurring the additional expense of re-shipping it to its original destination before the contents of the sixty packing cases were assembled, and even then with great difficulty because the working drawings were missing.[54]

The *Liverpool Standard's* description of this first church differs in some ways from that of the *Church of England Messenger*. The 'iron plates' which seemed to suggest a flat iron church of the Wesleyan type, turn out to be corrugated iron; the wall lining was simply strained canvas with granite paper, and the roof was lined with insulating felt. The church measured about 44ft. by 68ft., with a tower, a nave and two aisles, two galleries, communion table, pulpit and reading desk, a robing room and baptistery. The building could accommodate 650 people, but when packed would not exceed fifty tonnes measurement, or 2,000 cubic feet, the size of a moderate room.[55] After twenty years a stone church was built at Williamstown, and the iron building was removed to become the Sunday school of St Phillip's, Collingwood, where it remained until it was demolished early this century.[56]

A coloured lithograph of Hemming's works in August 1853 shows the second church for Melbourne [fig. 3.10]. This church was put up in 1855 under the supervision of the leading Melbourne architects Knight, Kemp & Kerr. It was destroyed by a storm in 1908.

The third of these churches, and the only one which survives, at least in part, was a much smaller structure,[57] probably of 600 sittings to judge from the price, and was put up on the fringes of the town of Gisborne, about 40 miles north-west of Melbourne.[58]

A few Hemming buildings went to other colonies, such as a Congregational

Fig 3.9 | Interior view of the second church erected for the Diocese of Melbourne at Hemming's Patent Improved Portable Buildings Manufactory, Bristol [State Library of Victoria].

Church in Sydney, and an Anglican vicarage, the fate of which is unknown. The characteristic which distinguishes Hemming's work from that of the earlier prefabricators is that the buildings are timber rather than iron-framed, which is much more like common shed construction, and much less industrialised in principle. This was the very point singled out for a criticism in *Instrumenta Ecclesiastica,* which must have been targeted at Hemming in particular:

> *It may be safely asserted that the iron churches, of which several have been sent out to the colonies, or erected as temporary churches at home, have not fulfilled these conditions. In fact their construction is merely a wooden one. Their framework is of wood, covered externally with corrugated iron; the pillars are wooden posts; and the roofs both of nave and aisles are wooden in their construction. What is such a building but a wooden structure encased in metallic plates?*[59]

Hemming transferred his business to his son, Samuel C. Hemming, and it moved from Bristol to London. Henceforward efforts were made to give the buildings more architectural qualities – sometimes Gothic, sometimes Tudorish and sometimes Italianate. St Paul's, a temporary church in the grounds of the vicarage at Kensington, opened on 30 October 1855, seating 800, the first iron temporary

Fig 3.10 | View of prefabricated iron church for Melbourne as it appeared in Hemming's manufactory yard, Bristol, 1853 [State Library of Victoria].

church in London. 'It would not be difficult', it was claimed, 'on a future occasion to give a more ecclesiastical character to such a structure externally.'[60] The Australian market had by now dried up, and most of Hemming junior's buildings were for domestic consumption, but a few were still exported.

The criticism of Hemming's churches had not been because they were iron, but because they were *not* iron, merely iron sheets on a timber frame. The Ecclesiological Society had taken a broad minded view of the prefabrication of churches, first persuading Peter Thompson to accept their advice on the ritual arrangement of his temporary structures, and then in 1853 commissioning R.C. Carpenter to design a model iron church.[61] Carpenter, however, became ill and died in 1855, and it was left to William Slater, Carpenter's pupil and successor, to design an iron church as it ought to be. Hemming seems to have taken this proposal so seriously as to have virtually copied Slater's design in a church which he was offering in 1862, whether he ever sold such churches remains a moot point.

The same sort of rethinking was forced upon another firm of prefabricators, Tupper & Carr. In 1858 they built an iron church in Westbourne Road, Islington, in six weeks,[62] but a correspondent of *The Builder* asked 'Surely something might be done to make their churches and chapels more worthy in architectural character?'[63] Tuppers responded to the effect that they were constrained by cost, and by the fact that the clergy were concerned with the inside rather than the outside. They had, however, now appointed G. Adam Burn as their architect, and he was preparing a series of designs for iron churches.[64] Burn had been a pupil of Thomas Hopper,[65] one of the earliest architects to engage with iron construction, and it is a pity that nothing more is heard of these designs. This was in fact a dead end. English bishops refused to consecrate iron structures as parish or district churches, so that they could only be set up for temporary use,[66] and that in turn meant that they were cheap and nasty.

Later we do see some attempt by Tuppers to Gothicise their churches, but it does little to disguise their fundamental cheapness. And this is now pretty much par for the course. A number of makers were producing rudimentary Gothic churches clad in corrugated iron, but this is barely relevant to our present theme because the truth is that far more of them were used in Britain than in the colonies. However, Francis Morton of Liverpool was something of an exception. Firstly, his St Mark's, Claughton, Birkenhead, is a substantial church, approaching ecclesiological standards.[67] Secondly, he advertised in Australia. In 1879 the Australian *Town and Country Journal* illustrated a number of the buildings then available from Morton, and reported that the company was represented by G.H. Royce and Co. of George Street, Sydney. Royce undertook that the buildings could be put up at a fixed cost to the purchaser at any location in Australia within one hundred miles of a railway station.[68] This may have been a considerable selling point, especially in Queensland, which was served by a number of separate lines running inland from the coast, but not linked in the north-south direction. Many of Morton's products are in fact found in Queensland – fences, gates and telegraph poles – but I know of no churches or other complete buildings.

Broadly speaking, when one does find a late nineteenth-century iron-clad church in Australia, it reflects a need for cheapness, just as in Britain, rather than a response to special colonial constraints. And one should not be too hasty in assuming that they were regarded as inferior. William Cooper made the remarkable claim of his church, catalogue number 206, that it was 'a much admired and approved design, being in strict accordance with the rules of modern architecture'.[69]

One has to go outside the Empire to see the route that the British could have followed if their congregations had not been so cheeseparing, and their Bishops so stubborn about consecrating iron churches. The Sveti Stefan (Aya Istefanos) Bulgarian Church, Istanbul, is a wonderfully exotic cast iron clad church in what is most nearly described as *rundbogenstijl*, made in Vienna, apparently in 1871.[70] Others, such as those made in Belgium to the design of Genaro Falacios, are found in the Philippines and Latin America.

I refer finally to an extreme case of church design adapting to special constraints. By the end of the nineteenth century much of Australia was almost as urban as Britain, but the city of Darwin at the north end of the continent was

Fig 3.11 | The Wesleyan church for Darwin at Simpsons' yard in Wakefield Street, Adelaide [photo courtesy Rev. Stafford].

Fig 3.12 | The Wesleyan church, Darwin, 1897: detail of the verandah with the composite hip rafter [Miles Lewis].

different, and still is today – remote, with an enervating tropical climate, and subject to cyclones [fig. 3.11]. The Wesleyan chapel at Palmerston (now Darwin) was destroyed by cyclone in February 1897 and, as the location fell within the ægis of the South Australian Conference, the South Australian Wesleyans subscribed for a new church. The church was built and possibly designed by A. Simpson & Son, metalware manufacturers, of Adelaide, and was assembled on their premises in Wakefield Street before being despatched in 1897.[71] A photograph of the building as erected in Adelaide shows it complete but for the ridge vent and the corner ties, while a photograph of it as built in Darwin shows these elements, the ties being apparently of wire, running diagonally to the ground.[72]

The whole of the framing is lightweight. The wall system comprises principal studs of cruciform section, between which run the pressed cladding sheets, which have a profile like weatherboarding. Behind this sheeting, at the centre of each panel, is a secondary stud which is not visible externally, and is a T section pointing inwards. The verandah is conceived more or less independently of the body of the building in that it is on a different module, and the common rafters are not continuous between the verandah and the main roof. The hip rafter, however, does appear to be continuous [fig. 3.12]. The wall module is 5ft. 6in. between principal studs, which may have been produced by the cladding sheet width being the same. The verandah columns, by contrast, are spaced at about 7ft. 6in. centres.

The hip rafter is a flat on edge, encased in sheet metal to produce a cruciform section with the side flanges angled downwards to conform to the geometry of the roof slopes to either side [fig. 3.13]. The cruciform section of the principal studs is formed similarly, and though I was not able to establish clearly that the core was a flat, this is my belief. The lightweight metal sheathing proves on examination to comprise two sheet metal covers of T section, one with the flange

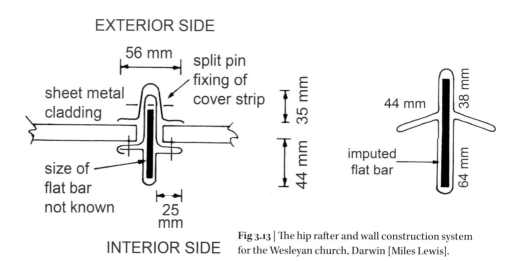

Fig 3.13 | The hip rafter and wall construction system for the Wesleyan church, Darwin [Miles Lewis].

pointing inwards, and the other the reverse. On the outside the junction of the wall sheeting at the stud is concealed by a cover strap which is also of T section, and is fixed onto the flange of the core member by means of split pins. The ridge piece is another iron bar, but not in this case wrapped up to form a cruciform section, and so particularly prone to buckling.

The system of construction used in the Knuckey Street church is too elaborate to have been devised for the specific building, and unlikely to have been developed even by a regular local prefabricator operating on a small scale. It seems likely that Simpsons imported the system, and given that the dimensions appear to be imperial, that it came from Britain or America. The latter seems more probable, for a very similar method of building up skylight bars from sheet metal wrapped around a flat bar was used there, and the cladding also suggests America.[73] Weatherboard profile cladding is not known to have been manufactured in Australia, whereas it was produced by at least half a dozen American manufacturers.[74]

There is no neat conclusion to be drawn from all this. It simply confirms that transferring a culture to an unfamiliar or even hostile environment is a sort of test tube experiment – a measure of its stamina and its flexibility. In the case of religious culture it is a double experiment, because preconceptions about correct form, orientation and detailing, are as powerful as practical considerations about comfort and efficiency and durability. What result are not just interesting compromises in design and technology, but interesting rationalisations, such as why a style like the Norman should be acceptable but the Italian should not, and why an iron frame should be acceptable but not a timber one. Nowhere are prejudices more enduring, or rationalisations more convoluted, than in the design of churches.

NOTES

1. See the watercolour of the 1850s reproduced in J. Kerr and J. Broadbent, *Gothic Taste in the Colony of New South Wales*, Sydney, 1980, p.72.
2. J.C. Loudon, *An Encyclopædia of Cottage Farm and Villa Architecture*, London, 1833.
3. Lady Franklin to Mrs Simpkinson, 7 September 1840, in G. Mackaness (ed.), *Some Private Correspondence of Sir John and Lady Franklin (Tasmania 1837–1845)*, 2 vols., Sydney, 1947, vol. 1, p.102.
4. See T. Mowl, 'The Norman Revival', in S. Macready and F.H. Thompson (eds.), *Influences in Victorian Art and Architecture*, London, 1985, p.45.
5. http://www.stclements.org.uk/oldsite/history.htm.

6. H. Colvin, *A Biographical Dictionary of British Architects 1600–1840*, New Haven and London, 2008, p.293.
7. Christ Church, Streatham, London, by J.W. Wild, 1840–2; ss Mary & Nicholas, Wilton, Wiltshire, by Wyatt & Brandon, 1840–6.
8. *The Ecclesiologist*, vol. 1, November 1841, pp.4–5. Salvin, who was charged with producing the New Zealand designs, was more than averagely versed in the Norman style, having spent four years in restoration work at Norwich Cathedral, and being currently responsible for the Cambridge Camden Society's restoration of the Church of the Holy Sepulchre, Cambridge. See J. Allibone, *Anthony Salvin: Pioneer of Gothic Revival*

Architecture 1799–1881, Columbia [Missouri], 1987, pp.12,115,116.

9. *Ecclesiologist*, vol. 1, November 1841, p.31. The Than model was available because it had been illustrated in A. C. Pugin and Le Keux, *Specimens of the Architecture of Normandy* (1827).

10. 'William Ayshford Sanford (1818–1902)', in J. Kerr (ed.), *The Dictionary of Australian Artists: Painters, Sketchers, Photographers and Engravers to 1870*, Melbourne, 1992, p.696. It was also noted by J. R. Wollaston that: 'Sandford's [sic] new school house is a very handsome, correct and costly building – would do well for a second church – more like one than a school, but badly placed.' See J.R. Wollaston, *Wollaston's Albany Journals (1848–1856)*, ed. C.A. Burton and P.U. Henn, Perth, 1954, p.228.

11. Fortuitously, their ecclesiological concerns intersected with a growing fashion for picturesque timber framed structures. There is no precise origin for the exposed frame (which appears to date from prehistoric times), but there is a specifically picturesque tradition in the eighteenth and nineteenth centuries. Barracks and other buildings for New Orleans designed by Louis-Pierre Le Blond de la Tour in 1723 show panels with criss-cross and diagonal bracing. In 1805 Charles Krafft published designs of two garden temples built in timber, one allegedly in the garden of the English king (presumably George III) at Westminster, and the other in the pleasure garden of a stadtholder in Holland. The frames were exposed and were largely divided into square panels, each containing either a single diagonal brace or a pair of crossed braces. This frame was filled rather than lined with timber pieces, but the members nevertheless stood proud of the surface and created the distinctive exposed frame effect. See Charles Krafft, *Plans, Coups et Élévations de Diverses Productions de l'Art de la Charpentier*, Paris, 1805, part 2, plate 3.

12. S.H. Brooks, *Designs for Cottage and Villa Architecture*, London, c.1839. Brooks illustrates three houses using exposed timber framing, between which is brick nogging plastered in different ways. Plates 1 to 3 show a sort of Tudor house, and 46 and 48 a rather vertiginous Swiss design, both with the framing in vertical panels, and with the brickwork roughcast. Plates 31 to 36 show a house purporting to combine the Elizabethan and Old English styles, with the brickwork plastered. Another house of a Tudorish character, 58 to 60, is perhaps meant to have the brickwork exposed. There is one house, 49 to 51, in what might be described as a Helvetio-Italianate manner, with broad panels in the frame intended to be filled with flint or ironstone. Another two houses are in the 'Old English' – a very pretty loopy barge-boarded Gothic style – 40 to 42 and 55 to 57, and are meant to be lathed between the framing, plastered inside, finished in Roman cement or mastic outside, and to have the cavity filled (rather unwisely) with sifted coal ashes, sawdust 'or any other substance which will absorb the moisture'.

13. J. Stacpoole, *Colonial Architecture in New Zealand*, Wellington, 1976, p.31.

14. *Instrumenta Ecclesiastica*, second series, London, 1856, plate 20.

15. For illustrations of William White's wooden church for the Diocese of Cape Town (1849), and E.S. Medley's Christ Church, St Stephen, New Brunswick (1863–4), see G.L. Hersey, *High Victorian Gothic: a Study in Associationism*, Baltimore, 1967, pp.85,90.

16. J.R. Wollaston, *Wollaston's Picton Journal*, ed. A. Burton, Nedlands, 1975, p.97. Within eight months the windows had been spoiled by neighbouring cattle (p.194).

17. Kerr and Broadbent, *op. cit.* [note 1], pp. 64,74.

18. A.E. Clark, *Church of Our Fathers: Being the History of the Church of England in Gippsland, 1847–1947*, Sale, 1947, p.64,73.

19. Watson has shown that Suter's work was rooted in the ecclesiological tradition in general and the Selwyn school in particular. Suter was at Cambridge in the 1840s, and is said to have obtained an MA degree from the university. He claimed to have been 'all his life connected with church matters', and in Watson's view was undoubtedly a member of the Cambridge Camden Society. His brother was ordained a deacon in 1855, whilst Bishop Selwyn was visiting Britain, and was later to become Bishop of Nelson, New Zealand. The Suters also maintained contact with Sampson Kempthorne, who had worked in Suter's father's office before migrating to New Zealand in 1841–2. See D. Watson, 'Outside Studding', *Historic Environment*, vol. 6:2&3, 1988, pp.28–9.

20. R. Sumner, 'The Queensland Style', in R. Irving (ed.), *The History and Design of the Australian House*, Melbourne, 1985, pp.300–1, based on illustrations in P. Hyndman and M. Baker, *An Approach to Queensland Vernacular Architecture*, Brisbane, 1975.

21. D. Watson, 'Models of Neat Architecture for Imitation' (undated typescript draft paper to the Australian Victorian Association), pp.3–4. This is Watson's opinion as revised from that expressed in his 'Outside Studding', *op. cit.* [note 20], pp.27–8.

22. *Ibid.* (Watson), p.30.

23. J. Cameron, *Centenary History of the Presbyterian Church in New South Wales*, 2 vols., Sydney, 1905, plate 94, as reproduced in N. Back, 'The Elphinstone Family', BArch Thesis, University of New South Wales, 1978, plate 28.

24. He appears first in a London directory of 1828 as a carpenter and builder opposite Cleveland Street, New Road, Regent's Park, and two years later was a bookseller in Osnaburgh Place, but in 1839 he had the temerity to submit a design for the new Houses of Parliament which was so poor that it was not even exhibited among the 87 unsuccessful entries. See I. Darlington, 'Thompson Fecit', *Architectural Review*, vol. 124, September, 1958, pp.187–8.

25. *The Builder,* vol. 11, August 1853, p.507.

26. *Colonial Magazine,* May 1841, p.12.

27. J. Stephens, *The Land of Promise: Being an Authentic and Impartial History of the Rise and Progress of the New British Province of South Australia*, London, 1839, advertising sheet (n.p.).

28. Stephens, 'The Land of Promise', advertising sheet in *op.cit.* [note 27] (n.p.)

29. *The Builder,* vol. 1, 18 March 1843, p.70.

30. Darlington, *op.cit.* [note 25], pp.187–8.

31. *Illustrated London News,* vol. 5, 7 September 1844, p.156. This probably amounted to a dispensation from fabricating houses in bond, which would otherwise have been necessary to avoid the duty on timber.

32. L. J. Ewens, 'The Establishment of Trinity Church Adelaide', a paper read at a meeting of the Pioneers' Association of South Australia, held at Trinity Church Hall, 6 July 1953, pp.5–7.

33. D. Pike, *Paradise of Dissent*, Melbourne, 1967, p.119.

34. T. Horton-James, *Six Months in South Australia; with some account of Port Phillip and Portland Bay*, London, 1838, advertisements, p.245.

35. Pike, *op. cit.* [note 34], p.265.

36. Ewens, *op. cit.* [note 33], pp.5–7.

37. *South Australian Register,* 21 July 1838.

38. *The Builder,* vol. 11, 6 August 1853, p.508.

39. One elevation is illustrated of a building which must be presumed to be the chapel, for it indicates a basilican cross-section with a high gabled nave lit by clerestory windows and flanked by lower side aisles. Both the facade articulated by the framework and the circular end window are broadly suggestive of S. Zeno Maggiore, Verona, but with two arched side doors rather than a central one, and with overall proportions more resembling those of Pistoia Cathedral, the general effect being a pleasing one. See *The Builder,* vol. 11, 20 August 1853, p.544. One portable brick house was sold by Dr Grace of Geelong in August 1853. It had been sent in twenty-two packages, presumably by Smallwood, and contained three rooms. No churches have been recorded. See P. Alsop, 'Prefabricated Buildings of the Nineteenth Century with especial reference to Geelong', typescript, Geelong, 1968, p.9.

40. *The Builder,* vol. 4, 18 April 1846, p.190. Thomas Edington appears in the catalogue of the International Exhibition of 1862 as an exhibitor of cast iron pipes, and Mr S.W. Johnston of the University of Glasgow Library informed me that the firm continued under the name of Thomas Edington & Sons, Phoenix Foundry, until in 1892 it ceased to appear in the Glasgow Directory.

41. *Journal de Liège* quoted in *The Builder,* vol. 7, 13 October 1849, p.487.

42. Philip Davies, *Splendours of the Raj,* London, 1985, p.10.

43. San Francisco Custom House records quoted in C.E. Peterson, 'Prefabs in the California Gold Rush, 1849', *Journal of the Society of Architectural Historians,* vol. 14:4, 1965, p.322.

44. *Liverpool Mercury,* 21 November 1851.

45. *Liverpool Mercury,* 7 July 1854.

46. B. Osborn, *A History of Holy Trinity Church, Bacchus Marsh,* Bacchus Marsh [Victoria], 1971, p.10.

47. G. Goodman, *The Church in Victoria during the Episcopate of the Right Reverend Charles Perry,* London, 1892, p.205.

48. Turner to Bishop Perry, printed in the *Church of England Messenger,* 1853, p.189, quoted in Lewis and Lloyd, 'Portable Buildings', pp.12–13.

49. *Church of England Messenger,* 1853, pp.251,189, quoted in *ibid.*

50. *Ibid.,* pp.13–14.

51. *Ibid.,* p.14. The Ven. Thomas Hart Davies had retired from his post at Melbourne on account of poor health. See Goodman, *op. cit.* [note 48], pp.192–3.

52. *Ibid.* (Goodman), p.207.

53. Circular reporting a church meeting of 25 July 1854, quoted in M. Read, 'Prefabricated Buildings and Structures', BArch Thesis, University of Melbourne, 1963, p.60.

54. Goodman, *op, cit.* [note 48], pp.207–8.

55. Quoted *Argus,* 3 September 1853, p.5.

56. Goodman, *op. cit.* [note 48], pp.207–8.

57. *Argus,* 24 August 1940.

58. In 1930 the church was moved to its present, more central position in Gisborne and re-opened for service. But in 1949 it was declared unsafe and was sold to the Eagley Woollen Mills, which rebuilt the roof, removed the tower, constructed a new brick facade at the west, and otherwise renovated the building. In 1961 it was re-purchased by the Church of England. See *The Age,* 28 June 1930; Read, *op.cit.* [note 54], pp 39–40; E.G. Robertson, *Victorian Heritage,* Melbourne, 1960, pp.48–9. There are some discrepancies between the accounts, especially in that Robertson erroneously dates the moving of the church to 1874.

59. *Instrumenta Ecclesiastica,* second series, London, 1856, caption to plate 66.

60. By Hemming & Co. of the Clift House works, Bow. *The Builder,* vol. 13, 27 October 1855, p.508.

61. H.-R. Hitchcock, *Early Victorian Architecture in Britain,* 2 vols., New York, 1972, vol. 1, p.528. See also H.-R. Hitchcock, 'Early Cast Iron Facades', *Architectural Review,* vol. 109, February 1951, p.113.

62. *The Builder,* vol. 16, 19 June 1858, p.428.

63. *The Builder,* vol. 16, 11 September 1858, p.622.

64. *The Builder,* vol. 16, 18 September 1858, p.640.

65. A. Felstead, J. Franklin and L. Pinfield, *Directory of British Architects 1834–1900,* London, 1993, p.137.

66. Hitchcock, *op. cit.* [note 62], p.528.

67. Both exterior and interior are illustrated in J. Steinhardt, *The Illustrated Guide to the Manufacturers, Engineers, and Merchants of England, Scotland, Ireland and Wales,* London, 1869, p.453.

68. 'Iron Buildings Illustrated and Described', *Town and Country Journal,* vol. 19, 1 March 1879, p.405.

69. *Illustrated Catalogue of Goods Manufactured and Supplied by W. Cooper Ltd.,* Horticultural Providers, London [c.1900], p.210.

70. There is a date of 1898 on the gate, but Bülent Özükan gives the date as 1871. See B. Özükan (ed.), *Türkiye'nin Kültür Hazineleri: Cultural Treasures of Turkey,* Istanbul, 2003, p.39.

71. A.W. Grant, 'Palmerston, The Northern Territory of Australia 1873–1899' (typescript 1983), p.3. See also P. Kelsey, 'Early History of the Palmerston (Darwin) Methodist Church', typescript, n.d., pp.3–5. The Rev. Arch Grant has advised me in 1995 that he has interviewed Mr Moxom Simpson, who is positive that his grandfather designed the building. Stafford believed the building to have been assembled in Pirie Street, however this is contradicted by

the company's centenary history, *Today not Tomorrow, a Century of Progress* (1954). See D. Marshall, Australian Heritage Commission file note (a), 10 January 1989.This states that the building was erected on a vacant lot in Wakefield Street, and elsewhere it makes reference to the existence a factory owned by the firm in Wakefield Street in the 1890s (pp.24–5) and to a two acre site there in 1894 (p.33). Marshall has observed that the factory buildings and fire tower in the background of the photograph suggest Wakefield Street as the location.

72. Photograph by McGann, 'Portable Iron Church for the Palmerston Wesleyan Congregation built by A Simpson & Son, Adelaide 1897', in the possession of the Rev. Stafford, cited in *ibid.* (Marshall). See also in the same reference 'Wesleyan Church and Parsonage', amongst general views of Darwin, Mortlock Library, Adelaide (Darwin 6 55, photograph B25069). A useful series of photographs are also reproduced in (Adrian Welke), *Former Methodist Church Plant, Knuckey St. Darwin, a statement of significance,* typescript report by Troppo Architects, no date (*c.*1980). Plate 1 shows the previous church and manse; plate 2 the subject building and the manse (dated at *c.*1900 on the ground of sparse vegetation); plate 3 the same at a later date (as the manse verandah had been built in and trees have grown; plate 4 the same buildings allegedly in 1955, but clearly before 1940 as the transepts are not in existence; and plate 5 a closer front view of the church itself, post World War II, with the transepts visible.

73. For the flat bar technology, see F.T. Hodgson et al, *Architecture, Carpentry, and Building,* 5 vols., Chicago, 1925–6, vol. 3, p.135 (Fig 148).

74. The Porter Iron Roofing and Corrugating Co. of Cincinatti, Ohio, published a catalogue in about 1885–90 including imitation weatherboard (or American 'clapboard') cladding. The Garry Iron and Steel Roofing Co. of Cleveland, Ohio, has nothing of the sort in its catalogue of about 1887, but in 1891 lists for the first time not only clapboard but imitation 'drop siding' [shiplap, or in Queensland 'chamferboard'] and brickwork. The Canton Steel Roofing Co. catalogue of 1899 also offered 'Weather-Board Siding' in lengths up to 10ft.; the Scully Steel & Iron Company was producing 'steel weatherboarding' in 1899; Mesker and Bro. of St Louis reportedly offered weatherboard profile sheet by about 1904; and the American Sheet and Tin Plate Company did so by 1906. See *Porter Iron Roofing and Corrugating Co.,* trade pamphlet, Cincinatti, n.d. (*c.*1885–90); Garry Iron and Steel Roofing Co., *Garry's Patent Iron and Steel Roofing,* Cleveland, 1891, pp.14–15; Garry Iron and Steel Roofing Co., *The Canton Steel Roofing Co.,* catalogue, Canton, 1899, p.32; Scully Steel & Iron Company, *Stock List,* Chicago, 1899, p.27; Mesker and Bro., *Mesker and Bro. Manufacturers of Complete House Fronts,* catalogue, St Louis, n.d. (*c.*1904), cited in Elton Engineering Books, *Catalogue Number 16,* London, 1999, p.50; and *'Sweet's' Indexed Catalogue of Building Construction,* New York, 1906, p.174.

4 · Experiments in Ecclesiology: Anglican Church Building in Colonial New Zealand

IAN LOCHHEAD

On 5 May 1839, the ship *Tory* sailed from Plymouth with the first contingent of New Zealand Company settlers bound for Port Nicholson, New Zealand. Four days later, on 9 May, a group of undergraduates at Cambridge University formed the Cambridge Camden Society.[1] Thus two great enterprises of the middle decades of the nineteenth century, the British colonisation of New Zealand and the reform of Anglican church architecture, can be said to have had their beginnings within the same week. The *Tory* arrived on 20 September and negotiation of land sales and preparation for the arrival of the main body of immigrants commenced. On 22 January 1840 the *Aurora* sailed into Wellington harbour with the main contingent of settlers and just over two weeks later, on 6 February 1840, the Treaty of Waitangi was signed between the British crown and the Maori tribes of New Zealand. British sovereignty was thus established in New Zealand, paving the way for the founding of further New Zealand Company settlements over the course of the next decade.[2]

By the end of 1839 the Cambridge Camden Society had over 100 members. The society was increasing in size rapidly, its influence was growing and it was already becoming involved with church restoration. With the launch of its journal, *The Ecclesiologist*, in 1841, the Society's commitment to colonial church building was clearly apparent; its very first article discussed church building in New Zealand.[3] If the foundation of New Zealand as a British colony and the establishment of the Ecclesiological Society were at first unrelated events, they were soon to evolve in tandem.

As a result of these events, Anglican church building in New Zealand was carried out according to ecclesiological principles virtually from its outset, making New Zealand, in a sense, the model ecclesiological colony. This produced a kind of experimental ecclesiology that is, if not unique, certainly unusual. As church builders in New Zealand grappled with fundamental problems of climate, materials and geology, along with the social and economic difficulties of the pioneering phase of the colony's development, they also had to contend with a challenging set of design principles and imperatives for church building laid down on the other side of the world. From the mid-1840s through to the end of the century, New Zealand church builders employed earth, timber, brick and stone to construct churches that expanded the definition of what might be considered an ecclesiologically correct church. When *The Ecclesiologist* stated in 1847 that

Fig 4.1 | Te Rangiatea Church, Otaki, 1848–51
[Lithograph by Charles Decimus Barraud].

57

'*If a church be of mud, it may still be a church*; properly arranged and suitable for Catholic worship', it is doubtful if anyone expected this to be taken literally.[4] In New Zealand, as we shall see, it was. Dogmatic assertions about the design of colonial churches were seldom helpful. The suggestion that Norman should be the style adopted for churches in New Zealand, because the grotesque forms of the carving would be compatible with the skills of Maori carvers, was never acted upon and the model church design based on Than Church in Normandy, sent to New Zealand in 1841, was never used.[5] By 1847 the Society had begun to realise that an experimental approach to colonial church building was essential.

> *We in England can only theorise; the Colonists might practically find what they are seeking ... What is wanted is that our Colonial fellow-Churchmen should learn Ecclesiology. Let them master this, and then they will be as competent to develop as we are, and will have every facility to do so. Even then they may make many blunders: but they will get experience from each trial, and will at length become perfect.*[6]

A key role in implanting ecclesiological principles in the new colony was played by George Augustus Selwyn (1809–78), the first and only Bishop of New Zealand. Selwyn was consecrated at Lambeth Place on 17 October 1841 and arrived in Auckland seven months later on 30 May 1842. Selwyn's interest in church building was apparent even before his arrival in the country and, as a patron of the Ecclesiological Society, his commitment to the new ideas about ritual and the architectural forms appropriate to it were never in doubt.[7] He immediately set about reforming the existing churches erected by the Church Missionary Society, starting with the CMS Chapel at Waimate in the north of the North Island (1838–42), where Selwyn was initially based. A sketch by Selwyn's chaplain, the Rev. W.C. Cotton, shows the interior of the chapel rearranged in collegiate form with the altar raised three steps above the principal floor level and the choir stalls aligned on either side of a central aisle. Even more radical was the apparent removal of ceiling boards above the sanctuary to reveal the timber framing of the roof, a recognition of the ecclesiological principle of structural reality.

Even when conducting services in largely unexplored parts of his episcopate during his extensive travels, Selwyn was conscious of the need to conduct worship in an appropriate fashion, as a sketch, reproduced in *The Ecclesiologist* showing the Bishop conducting a service for Maori on the shores of Lake Taupo in the central North Island, made clear.[8]

While based at Waimate, Selwyn lived in the CMS Mission House, and it was there that he planned St John's College, Auckland, the theological college which was to become the centre of his work in New Zealand. The College library still preserves the extensive collection of Ecclesiological Society publications sent to Selwyn, but it also contains a collection of Pugin's books that were donated to the library by Dr E.S. Hawtrey, the headmaster of Eton, where Selwyn had been a master prior to his departure for New Zealand.[9]

Selwyn's knowledge of and commitment to architectural design is confirmed by a portrait of him at work on the design of St John's College in a letter from Cotton in September 1844:

> For two days ... he [Selwyn] worked at the plans as steadily as tho' he had been an architect and nothing else – and before he gave over had not only the ground plan of the whole establishment drawn up, but also a beautiful general sketch of his idea of the whole – Mrs S[elwyn] looked in and admired – and turning to the frontispiece of one of Pugin's books, viz. an ecclesiastic in his study designing buildings, said 'there you are my dear'.[10]

A copy of Pugin's *True Principles* (1841), which contains the frontispiece referred to, is still in the College library. Further details were recorded in Cotton's journal.

> The Bishop hard at work as tho' he had been bred an architect planning St John's College, Bishop's Auckland ... He is going to send down [to Auckland] Pugin's works, and other books of architectural details, together with his plans that the architects may get correct details.[11]

Selwyn's sketches suggest that he had in mind an establishment resembling St Augustine's College at Canterbury (1844–73), but his ambitious plans were almost immediately frustrated by a shortage of skilled labour, the poor quality of building materials and difficulties with architects. Selwyn's frustration and disillusionment is clearly apparent in a journal entry for 23 June 1848.

> The buildings of the College have been constantly interrupted – at first by the failure of contractors in the distressed state of the Colony ... We first found ourselves deserted by the stone masons; and now it is difficult to procure carpenters, except at prices which we are unwilling to pay. We have, therefore, relinquished all building in stone; and after finishing such wooden buildings of a superior kind as were in hand, we now erect mainly temporary wooden sheds of the roughest kind, for such purposes as are absolutely necessary...I cannot therefore say much in praise either of the beauty or congruity of the College buildings, as necessity has repeatedly obliged us to change our style and the last change has been decidedly for the worse.[12]

Selwyn's experience with stone buildings was not a happy one; the two small stone churches built for him to designs by Samuel Kempthorne, St Stephen's, Judges Bay (1844) and St Thomas's, Tamaki (1844–45), deteriorated rapidly and had to be demolished. The one building that gave him some satisfaction was the St John's College chapel, 'a wooden building on stone foundations. The interior is exceedingly pleasing, and when filled with our Collegiate body, bears some faint resemblance to our College Chapels in England.'[13]

The St John's College Chapel, completed in 1847, was the most significant early example of the adaptation of ecclesiological principles to New Zealand conditions, and its genesis reveals the essentially experimental approach that Selwyn was forced to adopt once he realised that traditional ways of church building would not work [fig. 4.2]. The chapel was designed by Frederick Thatcher, an architect who had emigrated to the New Zealand Company's settlement at New Plymouth in 1843, and who subsequently moved to Auckland to take up a position in the Public Works department.[14] However, Selwyn's involvement was crucial from the outset and the building which resulted can more properly be described as the outcome of an ideal partnership between an ecclesiologically informed architect and an architecturally knowledgeable bishop.

Prior to his arrival at St John's, Thatcher had designed a primitive timber church with walls of vertical timber slabs at Te Henui, near New Plymouth in 1844, and a more sophisticated wooden chapel with exposed external framing for the CMS mission station at Maraetai in 1846. Both these buildings were considered to be temporary structures, a view that was almost universally applied to wooden buildings in 1840s New Zealand, but surviving illustrations suggest that they served as prototypes for the chapel at St John's College.[15]

Selwyn had already considered the possibilities of building in wood before he left England and the realities of New Zealand conditions caused him to revive these ideas.[16] Writing to his brother in April 1845 he elaborated on his earlier views:

> the churches of this country ... are chiefly of wood: though we have no reason to fear earthquakes of any consequence – a plan which is now being drawn by one of our own architects under my direction, will effectually, I think secure them against earthquakes and wind; the latter of which, is I think much more to be feared than the former. The main timbers of the roof are to rest on the ground, and to be concealed in the walls of the Porch and Transept so that the side walls will have little or no weight to support, and the whole will rest upon a base nearly twice as wide as the Church itself.[17]

Selwyn's idea of extending the roof trusses beyond the walls of the building to form buttresses was incorporated into the design of the St John's College Chapel, where they are visible in the walls of the porch and transepts. The plan, with its apsidal east and west ends, also owes much to Selwyn's influence and was derived from the Rev. J.L. Petit's *Remarks on Church Architecture* (1841), which illustrates medieval French churches with similar plans.[18] At a time when church architects in Britain were still primarily focussed on deriving their ideas from national sources, the introduction of French motifs at St John's illustrates the freedom to experiment that was possible in the colonial environment.

Thatcher's contribution to the design can be seen in its refined proportions and use of an exposed timber frame with a skin of vertical boards and battens applied to the inner surface of the frame, a system he had earlier used for the colonial hospitals in New Plymouth and Auckland, as well as the chapel at Maraetai [fig. 4.3]. With its cruciform plan, revealed construction, steeply pitched roof and cusped lancet windows, the St John's College Chapel established the basic pattern for ecclesiologically-inspired timber churches in New Zealand for the next three decades. Later churches differed from the St John's Chapel in one

Fig 4.2 | St John's College Chapel, Auckland, by Frederick Thatcher, 1847 [Archives, Diocesan School for Girls, Epsom, Auckland].

Fig 4.3 | St John's College Chapel, Auckland, by
Frederick Thatcher, 1847. [Auckland Public Library].

important respect, as a uniform skin of vertical boards and battens proved more robust than the picturesque but less durable exposed timber frame.

The St John's Chapel quickly became the heart of the college community, and its importance can be sensed in the description by Selwyn's friend, John Coleridge Patterson, first Bishop of Melanesia. It was, he wrote in 1855, like

> the inside of a really good ecclesiastical building in England ... a semicircular apse at the west, containing a large handsome font, open seats of course. The east end very simple, semicircular apse, no rails, the Bishop's chair on the north side, bench to the south. Here my eye and mind rested contentedly & peacefully. The little chapel, holding about seventy persons, is already dear to me.[19]

What may have seemed a very modest structure from a British perspective was seen very differently by churchmen in New Zealand.[20] Within the history of colonial ecclesiology it demonstrated the way in which ecclesiological principles could be adapted to timber construction a year before the publication of the Rev. William Scott's article 'On Wooden Churches' in *The Ecclesiologist*.[21]

For Thatcher, the design of churches was more than just a professional task, as soon after the completion of the chapel he began to prepare to take holy orders and in 1853 he was ordained priest, becoming the first vicar of St Matthew's parish in Auckland. As vicar he commissioned William Butterfield to design a new parish church, although this was never built.[22] He nevertheless continued to design churches for Selwyn, as well as the headmaster's house for the Church of England Grammar School in Auckland in 1857. This was constructed from local scoria stone and based on ecclesiological models for parsonage houses. More unconventional was Bishopscourt (1862) in Auckland and its associated library. Built of wood and clad in vertical board and battens, it was organised around a cloistered courtyard. The belfry linked to the cathedral library was a cause for mirth among some members of the clergy since, because the peal of bells intended for the unbuilt cathedral was too heavy to be suspended in the tower, they were hung from a stout framework at ground level, with an octagonal tower and spire above. The belfry was 'proof' according to the Rev. Richard Taylor 'that everything was reversed in the antipodes'.[23]

Thatcher's largest church was built in Wellington between 1864 and 1866, and there he applied all he had learned during twenty years as an architect in New Zealand [fig. 4.4]. Earthquakes in the region in 1848 and 1855 meant that there was no question of building in any other material than wood. In its original form St Paul's consisted of an aisled nave ending in an apsidal east end. The entrance was located beneath a western tower with a shingled spire, similar in form to that of the Cathedral Library in Auckland. The exterior, clad in vertical boards and battens, was plain with Early English details, but the interior, with its arcaded nave, spacious chancel and open timber roof, demonstrated that it was possible to create an impressive ecclesiastical space using the indigenous timbers of New Zealand. Nevertheless, contemporary descriptions of St Paul's downplayed its

Fig 4.4 | St Paul's Church, Wellington, by Frederick Thatcher, 1866 [Art History & Theory Visual Resources Collection, University of Canterbury].

timber construction, mentioning this almost as an afterthought: 'There is no redundancy of ornaments, and no pretension to the floridness of the early English architecture as applied to more extensive buildings; but a general neatness of design pleases the eye as being more appropriate to a sacred edifice constructed in wood.'[24] Like so many churches in colonial New Zealand, St Paul's was added to progressively over the years as the population expanded; a south transept was added in 1868 and one to the north in 1874, when the north aisle was also extended, each new section contributing to an impression of organic growth that was medieval in spirit. This additive approach had already been endorsed by the Ecclesiological Society in one of its most influential publications, *A Few Words to Church Builders*, which recognised that this 'way of building was often adopted by our ancestors ... with the happiest results; as it ought to be now in the Cathedral churches of Sydney, Montreal and Calcutta.'[25] As we shall see, it was not just cathedrals that would be constructed in this way in New Zealand.

The completion of St Paul's, Wellington, marks the end of the Selwyn phase of New Zealand church building, during which time the Bishop directly oversaw the construction of the first wave of Anglican churches throughout the country. After attending the 1867 Lambeth Conference Selwyn was appointed

Fig 4.5 | Design for a Chapel and School for Canterbury, by William Butterfield, 1850 [Anglican Diocesan Archives, Christchurch].

Bishop of Lichfield, a post he accepted with some reluctance. By that time the Diocese of New Zealand had been subdivided into sees in Auckland, Wellington, Christchurch and Dunedin. Selwyn's departure also brought an end to Thatcher's architectural career, as he accepted the position of private secretary to the Bishop and returned to England in 1868.

During the course of Selwyn's episcopate the rapid adoption of Christianity by Maori also resulted in new and innovative church designs. The most remarkable result of this new synthesis of indigenous building traditions and Gothic Revival forms occurred at Otaki in the south of the North Island. There, the great chief, Te Rauparaha, oversaw the building of Te Rangiatea, a large timber church in which the roof ridge was supported by columns hewn from single trees. Although there were Gothic precedents for a central colonnade of this kind, the form of Te Rangiatea derived from the carved meeting house or *whare whakairo*. In plan, the church was a simple rectangle, betraying the influence of the Church Missionary Society on its design rather than that of the Ecclesiologists. However, the extensive use of woven *tukutuku* panels and painted decoration on the walls and ceiling created an interior that rivalled High Victorian churches for decorative richness [fig. 4.1].[26]

By the time Te Rangiatea was completed in 1851, new church building

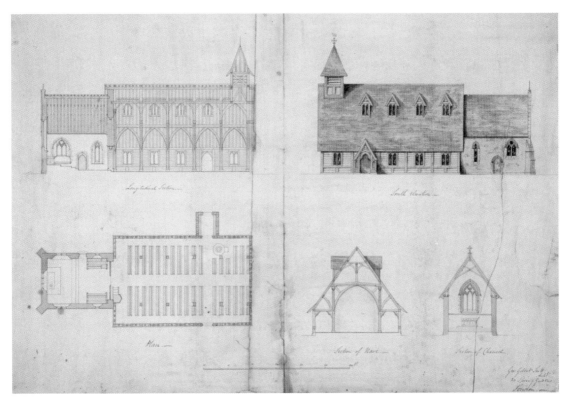

Fig 4.6 | Church for the Canterbury Settlement by George Gilbert Scott, *c.* 1850.
[Canterbury Museum, Christchurch, plan 286/7]

initiatives were underway in the South Island, where the Canterbury Association had established a Church of England Settlement in 1850. This was the last, the most ambitious, and certainly the most idealistic of all the New Zealand Company's settlements, and was intended to transplant to New Zealand a cross section of English provincial life, establishing a city with a full ecclesiastical hierarchy from bishop to parish clergy.[27] The ecclesiastical character of the settlement was reflected in the plan of the city of Christchurch, as the names of principal streets came from English, Irish and colonial bishoprics while two city squares were named after the martyrs of the English Reformation, Cranmer and Latimer.[28] The central square, initially known as Ridley Square, was later renamed Cathedral Square. In reality, the first bishop, J.H.C. Harper, did not arrive until 1857, initial church building encountered considerable difficulties and the promised cathedral was not completed until 1904. Yet if New Zealand can be described as the ideal ecclesiological colony, within that country Canterbury was the most complete ecclesiologically-inspired settlement.[29] From the beginning, efforts were made to establish church building on sound principles. In anticipation of the need for model designs capable of being adapted to multiple uses, the Canterbury Association commissioned a design for a chapel-school and master's house from William Butterfield in 1849, a year prior to the first settlers arriving in the colony [fig. 4.5].[30] Butterfield's design incorporated all three functions in a building that anticipated the later adaptability of local architects. The nave of the chapel doubled as a schoolroom and the master's house was arranged vertically to form a western tower, its domestic function signalled by the prominent chimneys on the south side. Although materials were not specified, it was clearly intended as a masonry building. However, by the time the 'Canterbury Pilgrims' (as the first settlers were known) arrived in 1850 it was recognised that timber would be the principal building material in the colony for some time to come.

This realisation is reflected in a design, dating from around 1851, by George Gilbert Scott for a parish church for the new settlement, in which the nave is of timber and the chancel, probably intended for later construction, was in stone [fig. 4.6].[31] Scott's design, with its arcaded nave and open timber roof, reflects his interest in medieval timber construction and, as the Rev William Scott pointed out in 1848, he was familiar with early timber churches such as St Oswald's, Lower Peover, in Cheshire. Neither Scott nor Butterfield's designs were built, although Scott returned to the idea of timber construction when he was commissioned to design the most important church in Canterbury, Christ Church Cathedral, in 1859.

The primitive nature of church building during Canterbury's early years is well illustrated by a design for a log church dating from 1852. The architect was Benjamin Mountfort (1825–98), a pupil of R.C. Carpenter who came to New Zealand with the first contingent of Canterbury colonists.[32] There is some evidence that Mountfort was at least the semi-official architect of the new settlement (he was described as 'the architect of Canterbury' in 1853), and his architectural credentials certainly equipped him for this role. He was an admirer of Pugin, was well versed in ecclesiological theory and he became one of the leading High Church laymen in the diocese. Mountfort's Hemingford church was to be constructed from vertical log walls with a steeply-pitched, open timber roof. Surprisingly for a church of such primitive character, the tracery was Decorated in style, although Mountfort adopted Early English details for his later churches. He probably knew William Scott's essay on timber churches, which commended the vertical log walls of the timber Anglo Saxon church at Greensted in Essex for expressing the Christian virtue of heavenward aspiration, while condemning the horizontal log construction of some North American churches as inappropriate for ecclesiastical buildings.[33] The Hemingford church was intended to function eventually as the chancel of a much larger church of masonry construction, and it was probably anticipated that the log structure would also be replaced when the size of the parish and the availability of resources increased. Mountfort's approach was thus the reverse of Scott's, who proposed building a timber nave first and adding the stone chancel later.

There is, however, little evidence that Mountfort's log church was actually built, or if it was, its life was short. Better documented is Holy Trinity, Lyttelton (1852–53), the colony's first church. This was also designed by Mountfort, who utilised traditional English timber frame construction with an infill of brick nogging. Mountfort was thus reverting to a type of vernacular construction that had not been used for churches in Britain since the late Middle Ages. Only half of Mountfort's ambitious design was erected, but the tall, aisled nave dominated other buildings in the fledgling town. The Trinitarian symbolism of its timber framing, particularly evident in the trio of triangles that formed the west gable, was a clear signal to all those arriving in Canterbury of the central position that the Anglican Church occupied in the life of the settlement.[34]

Holy Trinity's domination of the Lyttelton townscape was to prove short-lived. Mountfort had made the fatal mistake of assuming that building techniques and materials that worked under English conditions would also apply in New Zealand. However, his adaptation of green oak timber framing produced disastrous results when applied to local timbers, which shrank and warped. The church was shaken by high winds, the brick nogging worked lose and the congregation rapidly lost confidence in the building. Eventually the church was dismantled in 1857 and replaced in 1860 by a new building constructed of locally-quarried scoria to designs by George Mallinson.[35] The first Holy Trinity, Lyttelton, is one of the most dramatic demonstrations of the perils of building with untried materials in an unfamiliar environment, and of the dangers of adapting construction practices from one part of the world to another without proper testing.

In spite of the failure of Holy Trinity, Mountfort continued to receive ecclesiastical commissions, and it is not surprising that in his 1855 design for St Bartholomew's, Kaiapoi, an outlying settlement to the north of Christchurch, he adopted Selwyn's system of continuing the roof trusses down to ground level to form buttresses. Selwyn himself visited the small timber church in 1856 and must have been gratified to find his ideas about church design adopted in Canterbury. As a pupil of Carpenter, Mountfort was almost certainly aware of the former's design for a timber church for Tristan da Cunha, published in the second series of *Instrumenta Ecclesiastica* (1856), one of the Ecclesiological Society's most important publications and one specifically intended to provide models for the colonial church. Mountfort's belfry at Kaiapoi has much in common with Carpenter's design and he also employed exposed timber framing, also seen in the Tristan da Cunha church.

The influence of Carpenter's model designs can also be detected in Mountfort's St John's Church, Heathcote, a parish to the east of Christchurch. St John's was built in 1857 and is significant as probably the earliest earth-built church in New Zealand [fig. 4.7]. Although Carpenter's Chapel School was never intended as a model for a building of cob construction, its forms translated readily into the more primitive material, though Mountfort employed stone for the dressings to doors and windows. Mountfort probably took considerable satisfaction in demonstrating that a church built of earth could indeed be 'properly arranged and suitable for Catholic worship'.[36]

Cob churches were never intended to be long-term structures, but St John's survived until 1892 when it was replaced by a wooden building, which itself was never completed. However, St Cuthbert's Church at Governor's Bay, at the head of Lyttelton Harbour, demonstrated the durability of cob construction. Designed by George Mallinson and built in two stages in 1860 and 1875, when the chancel was added, the church has survived to the present day, although it suffered serious earthquake damage in 2010.

Experiments with a diverse range of building materials, ranging from earth, vertical logs, timber framing with brick infill and local volcanic stone, all proved to be unsatisfactory in one way or another. By the late 1850s Mountfort had arrived at a similar conclusion to Frederick Thatcher a decade earlier, that vertical board and batten construction over an internal timber frame was the most

Fig 4.7 | St John the Evangelist's Church, Heathcote, by Benjamin Mountfort, 1857–59 [A.C. Barker Collection, Canterbury Museum, Christchurch].

Fig 4.8 | St Mary's Church, Halswell, by Benjamin Mountfort, 1862 [A.C. Barker Collection, Canterbury Museum, Christchurch].

Fig 4.9 | St Michael and All Angels' Church, Christchurch, by William FitzJohn
Crisp, 1872 and belfry, by Benjamin Mountfort, 1861 [Ian Lochhead].

efficient, economical and adaptable form of construction for parish churches
in New Zealand. First at St Peter's, Riccarton, in 1857, and later at St Mary's,
Halswell, in 1862, he consolidated his approach to timber-gothic church design
and established models that would serve for the rest of his career [fig. 4.8]. An
open timber porch led into a nave, sometimes with single or double aisles, de-
pending on the amount of accommodation required. A spacious chancel with the
altar against the east wall provided an appropriate setting for worship, while the
open timber roof acknowledged the ecclesiologists' requirements for reality in
construction. Windows of simple lancet form illuminated the nave, with timber
tracery reserved for the east window above the altar. He also adopted the principle of picturesque utility that allowed for the clear expression of the functional
relationship of the church's individual components to the whole. Although the
architectural means were limited, the expression of ecclesiological principles
was not compromised.[37]

One of Mountfort's most experimental designs was the free-standing timber
belfry (1861) for the mother church of the Christchurch Diocese, St Michael and
All Angels.[38] The church itself was little more than a timber shed, but Mountfort's
design performed the dual roles of lychgate and belfry. It drew inspiration from
both the timber belfries of Essex as well as the free-standing wooden belfries of
Norway, published in the second series of *Instrumenta Ecclesiastica* (1856). The
unusual Rhenish helm roof, a reference to the Anglo Saxon tower of St Mary,
Sompting, in Sussex, evoked the early history of English church architecture, an
appropriate reference during the founding years of the church in New Zealand.
But even in Christchurch the belfry was seen by some as an aberration. J.E.

FitzGerald, the first Provincial Superintendent of Canterbury, and an informed amateur architect, wrote that:

> they have set up the bell I sent out on a tower and a gateway near the church which is something like the pagoda in which men in Greek capes and gold tassels play trombones in Mt Cromorne and other gardens. Mountfort appears to suffer under fits of temporary architectural insanity for in lucid intervals he is good enough ... .[39]

The original St Michael's was replaced in 1872 by the large timber church with Early French details that still stands on the site [fig. 4.9]. It was the remarkable first design of a little-known architect, William FitzJohn Crisp, a pupil and assistant of Robert Speechly, the supervising architect for George Gilbert Scott's Christ Church Cathedral.[40] With its clearly expressed timber frame, robust brackets and clerestory of rose windows, St Michael's is a translation in timber of muscular High Victorian Gothic. One of New Zealand's largest and finest timber Gothic churches, it served as the pro-cathedral until the completion of the first stage of Scott's Christ Church in 1881.

Among nineteenth-century churches in New Zealand, Scott's cathedral for Christchurch is one of the most fascinating.[41] Having already supplied a design for a parish church for the settlement, and as one of the most prolific designers of Victorian churches, Scott was an obvious choice as cathedral architect, although some Cantabrians, FitzGerald among them, believed that a local architect should have received the commission. Scott had already designed a cathedral for St John's in Newfoundland, so was aware of the difficulties of working in remote locations. He also knew about the dangers posed by earthquakes in New Zealand and his initial proposal specifically addressed this problem by supporting the roof on an internal timber framework that was a development of the arcaded nave with flanking aisles used in his earlier parish church design. As was fitting for a cathedral, a clerestory, also constructed from timber, rose above the aisle roofs [fig. 4.10]. This massive timber frame was enclosed by stone walls to the aisles and east and west ends. A north-west tower, with a timber-framed, broach spire, completed the design. In style the building was more Early French than English in character, reflecting the stylistic shifts within Victorian architecture of the 1850s and early 1860s. Bishop Harper's Commissary, the Rev. Thomas Stevens, saw the plans in Scott's office in January 1862 and became an enthusiastic advocate: 'I think that the design is very beautiful and original. The columns in the nave are to be single trees running up to the plate of the clerestory. It will be worth a voyage to New Zealand to see if it is ever executed.'[42]

The sources of Scott's design have been the subject of considerable discussion. He was no doubt aware of an earlier hybrid timber and stone design made for New Zealand by Henry Woodyer, described in *The Ecclesiologist* in 1850. These plans were to be taken to New Zealand by the Rev. Charles Abraham, a future Bishop of Wellington, and showed 'a church to be built, as to its walls, with rubble stone, no dressed work at all being required with internal arcades and the tracery to all the windows of wood. This is a happy idea, and was, we thought so far as the woodwork was concerned – ingeniously carried out.'[43] Scott would thus have been able to proceed with his cathedral design confident of the approval of the Ecclesiological Society.[44]

The use of timber arcades within stone buildings had occurred in medieval churches, but by the mid-nineteenth century there were few surviving examples. The best examples of large-scale medieval timber framing were found in tithe barns, such as those at Harmondsworth in London, which Scott had visited and sketched, and Great Coxwell in Berkshire, where the same combination of timber structure and stone exterior could be found that Scott was proposing for Christchurch's cathedral.[45] By the time he came to design the cathedral he already had experience in erecting a substantial building of similar construction, the dining hall of Bradfield College in Berkshire (1856).[46] It is, nevertheless, worth asking whether Scott would have used a timber frame for the dining hall at Bradfield had he not already designed a timber church for New Zealand five years earlier.

Reactions to Scott's design from Canterbury were, however, unfavourable. From the start Bishop Harper was opposed to the extensive use of timber, viewing it as inappropriate for a cathedral. With the completion of the railway to the Port Hills in 1863, building stone became more readily available and at a cost that was estimated as being half that of timber, which would have to be shipped from Auckland. Concerns about the threat of earthquakes were set aside and Scott agreed to provide an alternative design for internal columns, arcade and clerestory in stone. Construction began in 1864 under the supervision of Robert Speechly, but proceeded little further than the foundations. When Anthony Trollope visited Christchurch in 1872 he commented on 'the empty space with all the foundations of a great church laid steadfast beneath the surface. I could not but be melancholy as I learned that the honest, high-toned idea of the honest, high-toned founders of the colony would probably not be carried out.'[47]

Trollope's gloomy prediction was to prove unfounded, as a year later work on the cathedral recommenced. At this point Mountfort, now appointed supervising architect, reopened the question of returning to Scott's hybrid timber and stone design, since, as he explained in a letter to Scott,

> After having been unmolested for about twelve years, we have been subjected for two years together, to shock of earthquake of a more violent character than have been felt here since the foundation of the settlement ... with tall isolated columns [in the cathedral] made up of many stones and carrying arches exerting a pressure, I must confess I should not feel comfortable as to the possible consequences of any movement in the substructure.[48]

Scott responded positively to Mountfort's request and introduced a further modification to his original design, substituting decorative timberwork for the original stone gable on the west front above the rose window.

Yet in spite of renewed seismic activity in the region, the Cathedral Commission's preference for using stone won out, the final decision being taken on the advice of the Christchurch architect, W.B. Armson. With considerably longer experience of working in the colony, Mountfort remained uneasy about the use of stone and his concerns would ultimately prove well founded.[49] Scott's role as architect also shows him in a very different light from the popular perception of him as an unadventurous designer at the head of an architectural factory that churned out commonplace buildings.[50] From 1859 to 1873 he revealed himself as innovative, adaptable and sensitive to local requirements. For one of Britain's most celebrated architects, he also demonstrated remarkable patience with delays, changes of plan and the propensity of his colonial clients to ignore his advice. At the time of his death in 1878 the cathedral was still under construction. The tower and nave were completed in 1881 and, with a temporary wooden chancel in place, it was consecrated on All Saints day that year. The transepts and stone chancel were finally completed in 1904, but in its final form Christ Church Cathedral revealed little of the creative and experimental thinking that had underpinned its origins.

The fact that it took over forty years for Christ Church Cathedral to be built was typical of colonial church building. What makes the cathedral project unusual is the consistency of vision that was maintained over this extended time period. Much more characteristic is the sequence of events that occurred in the Christchurch parish of Avonside. Between 1855 and 1907 Holy Trinity church evolved in stages from a building of earth construction to one of stone.[51] The original building, probably designed by C.E. Fooks, was built of cob in 1855. At the time it was described as the 'only really substantial ecclesiastical building in Christchurch", but this was scant praise.[52] In 1869 Mountfort added a vestry and bell turret of vertical board and batten construction to the west end of the cob nave.

This incongruous combination of forms and materials was compounded when, as a result of a generous gift from a parishioner, Mountfort added a stone chancel to the east end of the cob church. The chancel and transepts were intended as the first stages of a permanent building and represented a new departure in Anglican church architecture in the diocese. The interior of the chancel was richly decorated with encaustic tile panels on the lower walls with bands of painted and stencilled decoration above. The floor was also covered with encaustic tiles, metalwork was executed by Hardman of Birmingham, and the windows made by Lavers and Barraud. The entire decorative scheme was designed by Mountfort. As an example of High Victorian ecclesiastical design, the chancel at Avonside was unique in New Zealand. For the next thirty years, however, the congregation contemplated this polychromatic splendour from the humble cob nave of the 1855 church. Only in 1905 was a new nave designed by Cyril Mountfort and the church was finally completed in 1907. Cyril Mountfort had worked as an assistant to his father, Benjamin, and had overseen the completion of Christ

Church cathedral. He was, therefore, familiar with Scott's plans and the nave he designed for Avonside was a scaled-down version of Scott's initial cathedral concept, although without a clerestory. In the earthquakes of September 2010 and February 2011 it performed just as Scott hoped it would; although the exterior stone walls were badly damaged the timber frame held firm and the roof remained in place.[53]

Not every colonial church was constructed in such a piecemeal fashion. St Luke's Church in Oamaru was designed by Edward Rumsey in 1864 and built from the abundant local limestone. Although Rumsey did not supervise construction, his design was followed with remarkable fidelity, an unusual procedure at a time when changing circumstances frequently led to projects being abandoned or significantly modified.[54] Rumsey was a pupil of George Gilbert Scott, and although he had been in the Australasian colonies since 1854 he had clearly kept himself informed of developments in church building in Britain.[55] The narrow site meant that the church has only a single aisle, but the interior of St Luke's exhibits the same level of consistency as the exterior and makes effective use of the natural qualities of the local limestone.

The persistent desire to build in what were regarded as permanent materials led to the construction of increasing numbers of churches in brick and stone as the nineteenth century drew to a close. In 1884 Mountfort was commissioned to design St John's Cathedral in Napier, on the east coast of the North Island.[56] Although he expressed reservations about the wisdom of building in brick in an area known to be prone to earthquakes, his concerns were not heeded. Taking his

Fig 4.10 | Christ Church Cathedral, Christchurch, west elevation & section, by George Gilbert Scott, 1873 [Anglican Diocesan Archives, Christchurch].

Fig 4.11 | St Mary's Pro Cathedral, Auckland, by Benjamin Mountfort, 1886–98 [Art History & Theory Visual Resources Collection, University of Canterbury].

cue from Albi Cathedral, the most admired example of a brick Gothic cathedral, Mountfort incorporated massive internal buttresses at St John's. In doing so he was responding to recent developments in English church architecture, such as G.F. Bodley's St Augustine's, Pendlebury (1870–74), J.L. Pearson's St Augustine's, Kilburn (1871) and Edmund Scott's St Bartholomew's, Brighton (1872–4), but he almost certainly hoped that this structural device would be beneficial in the event of an earthquake. When Napier was struck by a magnitude 7.9 earthquake in February 1931 these precautions proved ineffectual and St John's Cathedral was destroyed along with the entire city centre.

Mountfort's final commission for a church of cathedral scale came from Auckland and was built as a pro-cathedral on land adjacent to the site selected by Bishop Selwyn for his cathedral in the 1840s. Although on this occasion there were discussions about building in brick or stone, and Mountfort even produced sketch designs for a stone cathedral, for reasons of economy timber became the final choice. St Mary's Pro Cathedral was built in two stages between in 1887 and 1898, although Mountfort did not live to see the completion of his last and greatest timber church.[57]

St Mary's exterior walls are of vertical board and batten and the windows push up into the roof to form a series of gables at the east end and along both sides of the nave. The simplicity of the exterior provides no hint of the dramatic quality of the timber interior [fig. 4.11]. The metaphor of the church as the ship of souls is nowhere more in evidence than here, with the apsidal east end as the prow and the unbroken line of the roof ridge as the keel. This was a metaphor that William Scott had adduced in his 1848 article on timber churches and it is certainly one that Mountfort must have had in mind. By using the aisles to buttress the nave, Mountfort was able to eliminate the collar beams that were a consistent feature of earlier timber church designs, creating a structure in which every element aspires towards the vertical. It is a building in which truth to materials, reality of construction and liturgical appropriateness harmonise to create a unique space for worship.

The experimentation with different materials and systems of construction, the anxieties about high winds and earthquakes, and the disjunctions that resulted from continually interrupted building programmes are resolved at St Mary's in a building that is coherent in design, well adapted to local conditions, and, as far as liturgical requirements were concerned, judged by contemporaries as 'superior to anything of the kind in Auckland'.[58] What is more, it did not rely on the tradition of medieval timber framed construction using collar ties and king posts employed by Scott and others for their colonial churches. This was an original colonial solution to the idea of a large timber church, and as such it provided a fitting climax to the development of ecclesiologically-inspired church building in colonial New Zealand.

NOTES

1. On the origins of the Ecclesiological Society see James F. White, *The Cambridge Movement: The Ecclesiologists and the Gothic Revival*, Cambridge, 1962, pp.25ff. See also Geoffrey K. Brandwood, '"Fond of Church Architecture" – the Establishment of the Society and a Short History of its Membership', in C. Webster and J. Elliott (eds.), *'A Church as it Should Be': The Cambridge Camden Society and Its Influence*, Stamford, 2000, pp.45–61.

2. For the role of the New Zealand Company see P. Burns, *Fatal Success: A History of the New Zealand Company*, Auckland,1989.

3. 'Parish Churches in New Zealand', *The Ecclesiologist*, vol. 1, November 1841, pp.4–5.

4. 'Church Building in the Colonies', *The Ecclesiologist*, vol. 7, January 1847, p.16.

5. 'Parish Churches in New Zealand', *op. cit.* [note 3], p.4 and 'New Zealand', *The Ecclesiologist*, vol.2, November 1841, p.31.

6. 'Church Building in the Colonies', *op. cit.*, p.15.

7. On Selwyn's influence on church building in New Zealand see Jonathan Mane-Wheoki, 'Selwyn Gothic: The Formative Years', *Art New Zealand*, vol. 54, 1990, pp.194–204 and 'Selwyn the Ecclesiologist – in theory and practice' in Allan K. Davidson (ed.), *A Controversial Churchman: Essays on George Selwyn, Bishop of New Zealand and Lichfield and Sarah Selwyn*, Wellington, 2011, pp.128–45.

8. *The Ecclesiologist*, vol. 5, March 1845, n.p. In a note to plate 1 'the Bishop of New Zealand using his canoe for an altar', *The Ecclesiologist* observed 'Of course we think the Bishop ought rather to have carried a *portatile* altar; but sure we are that his sacrifice was as acceptable as if it had been offered at the most gorgeous shrine human piety ever dedicated to GOD' (p. 86).

9. See Ian Lochhead, 'British Architectural Books in Colonial New Zealand', *Turnbull Library Record*, vol. 34, 2001, pp.31–4 and Mane-Wheoki, *op. cit.* [note 7 (2011)], pp. 137–8.

10. W.C. Cotton to his sisters, 9 September 1844, 'Correspondence of W.C. Cotton', microfilm, Auckland Museum Library.

11. W.C. Cotton, 'Journal', 4 September 1844, microfilm, Auckland Museum Library.

12. G.A. Selwyn, *Church in the Colonies No. xx: New Zealand, Part V. A Journal of the Bishop's Visitation tour Through his Diocese... in the Year 1848*, London, 1848), p.14.

13. *Ibid.*, p.17.

14. For a detailed account of Thatcher's career see Margaret Alington, *An Excellent Recruit: Frederick Thatcher – Architect, Priest and Private Secretary in Early New Zealand*, Auckland, 2007.

15. See Mane-Wheoki, *op. cit.* [note 7].

16. This was to be 'a new style of building suitable to New Zealand. A log house but of a different description. The ribs of the roof and walls being the same and resting on the ground.' Caroline Palmer, *Account of the last Days in Eton of George Augustus and Sarah Selwyn* (1841), quoted in Margaret Alington, *Fredrick Thatcher and St Paul's: An Ecclesiological Study*, Wellington, 1965, p.44.

17. G.A. Selwyn to W. Selwyn, Waikanae, 24 April 1845 in 'Letters of Bishop Selwyn and Others, 1842–67', 3 vols, typescript, Alexander Turnbull Library, Wellington, vol. 3, p.567.

18. See Sarah Selwyn, *Reminiscences by Mrs S.H. Selwyn, 1809–67*, ed. Enid Evans, Auckland, 1961, p.30.

19. C.M. Younge, *The Life of John Coleridge Patteson*, 2 vols.,London, 1874, vol. 1, p.209.

20. For a discussion of contemporary responses to Gothic Revival buildings in New Zealand see Ian Lochhead, 'Remembering the Middle Ages: Responses to the Gothic Revival in Colonial New Zealand', in J. Anderson (ed.), *Crossing Cultures: Conflict/Migration/Convergence. Proceedings of the 32nd Congress of the International Committee for the History of Art*, Melbourne, 2009, pp.536–40.

21. William Scott, 'On Wooden Churches', *The Ecclesiologist*, vol. 6, August 1848, pp.14–27.

22. 'S. Matthew's, Auckland', *The Ecclesiologist*, vol. 19, 1858, pp.91–2.

23. Richard Taylor, *The Past and Present of New Zealand with Its Prospects for the Future*, London, 1868, p.94.

24. *New Zealand Advertiser*, 7 February 1866, quoted in Alington, *op. cit.* [note 14], p.212.

25. Cambridge Camden Society, *A Few Words to Church Builders*, Cambridge, 1841, p.9. New Zealand was added to the list of cathedrals in the second edition of 1842.

26. For a detailed study of Maori church building see, Richard A. Sundt, *Whare Karakia; Maori Church Building, Decoration and Ritual in Aotearoa New Zealand 1834–1863*, Auckland, 2010. See also, Deidre Brown, 'The Maori Response to Gothic', *Architectural History*, vol. 43, 2000, pp.253–70.

27. For an account of the origins of the Canterbury Settlement see L. C. Webb, 'The Canterbury Association and its Settlement', in *A History of Canterbury*, 3 vols., Christchurch, 1957–71, vol. 1, pp.135ff.

28. J.P. Morrison, *Evolution of a City*, Christchurch, 1948, p.13.

29. For a discussion of the links between the Canterbury Association and the Ecclesiological Society see, Ian Lochhead, *A Dream of Spires: Benjamin Mountfort and the Gothic Revival*, Christchurch, 1999, pp.48–9. See also Brian Carrell, 'Singing the Lord's song in a strange land: Worship', in Colin Brown, Marie Peters & Jane Teal (eds.), *Shaping a Colonial Church: Bishop Harper and the Anglican Diocese of Christchurch*, Christchurch, 2006, pp.111–137.

30. Canterbury Association Minute Books, 8 December 1849, Christchurch Diocesan Archives. Butterfield's plans are also held in the Christchurch Diocesan Archives.

31. See J.N. Mané, 'Gilbert Scott's Colonial Churches', in M. Belcher and H. Debenham (eds.), *Australasian Victorian Studies Association: Conference Papers*, Christchurch, 1987, pp.31–42.

32. For an account of Mountfort's career see Lochhead, *op. cit.* [note 28]. Although Mountfort was not a member of the Ecclsiological Society he clearly knew their publications; his copy of volume one of *The Ecclesiologist* is now in the Alexander Turnbull Library, Wellington.

33. There was considerable interest in designing churches with walls of vertical logs around 1850, probably linked to recent interest in St Andrew's, Greensted. *The Ecclesiologist* reported, not entirely favourably, on the design of a church for Otago in New Zealand by Mr Hugall of Cheltenham, the walls to be made from 'trunks of trees, vertically in rows' but this was considered 'unnecessarily primitive.' See 'S. ––––, Otago', *The Ecclesiologist*, vol. 12, 1851, p.233.

34. For a detailed discussion of Holy Trinity, Lyttelton see Lochhead, *op. cit.* [note 28], pp.66–76.

35. The problems of Holy Trinity were far from over; the soft red scoria proved to be susceptible to weathering and required continual replacement. Destabilised by earthquakes in September 2010 and February 2011, it collapsed completely in an aftershock in June 2011.

36. In 1849 *The Ecclesiologist* included articles on both *pisé* (rammed earth) and cob construction. See 'Pisé Building', *The Ecclesiologist*, vol. 6, February 1849, pp.217–20; and 'Pisé and Cob Building', *The Ecclesiologist*, vol. 6, April 1849, pp.287–89.

37. In a survey of New Zealand architecture in 1900 Mountfort's small timber churches were described as 'notable examples of simple, honest construction, leading to the most pleasing results ... each has some special feature making it distinctive; yet in all there is an expression of individual feeling, giving them – simple and inexpensive though they are – a high place among our architectural works'. S. Hurst Seager, 'Architectural Art in New Zealand', *Royal Institute of British Architects Journal*, 3rd, series, vol. 7, 1900, p.484.

38. See Lochhead, *op. cit.* [note 28], pp.87–8.

39. J.E. FitzGerald to H. Selfe, 4 November 1861, Selfe papers, Canterbury Museum Library, quoted in E. Bohan, *'Blest Madman': FitzGerald of Canterbury*, Christchurch,1998, p.201.

40. See Jonathan Mané, 'St Michael and All Angels: A Colonial High Victorian Gothic Church', in M. Peters (ed.), *Christchurch – St Michael's: A Study in Anglicanism in New Zealand*, Christchurch, 1986, pp.194–204. For Speechly and Crisp, see Jonathan Mane-Wheoki, 'Brief Careers in Christchurch', *New Zealand Historic Places*, vol. 67, March 1998, pp.28–31.

41. For an account of the building of Christ Church Cathedral, see Lochhead, *op. cit.* (1999), pp.128–56. See also Robin Skinner, 'Drawing from an Indigenous Tradition? George Gilbert Scott's First Design for Christchurch Cathedral, 1861–62', *Architectural History*, vol. 53, 2010, pp.245–70.

42. *Church Quarterly Paper*, vol. 1, no. 3, April 1862, p.19.

43. 'New Churches: S. -----, New Zealand', *The Ecclesiologist*, vol. 11, 1850, pp.262–3.

44. On Scott and the Ecclesiological Society see Gavin Stamp, 'George Gilbert Scott and the Cambridge Camden Society', in Webster and Elliott, *op. cit.* [note 1], pp.173–89.

45. G.G. Scott, *Remarks on Secular and Domestic Architecture*, 2nd. ed., London, 1858, p.135. Scott also mentions the thirteenth-century aisled barns at Ely and Peterborough, both of which are now destroyed.

46. Skinner, *op. cit.* [note 40], p.252

47. Anthony Trollope, *Australia and New Zealand*, 2 vols., London, 1873, vol. 2, p.374.

48. B.W. Mountfort to G.G. Scott, 20 October 1873. Cathedral Commission, Inward Correspondence, Treasurer. Christchurch Diocesan Archives, Christchurch.

49. In the earthquake of 22 February 2011 the stone spire of Christ Church Cathedral collapsed and the west gable was badly damaged. Subsequent aftershocks have further damaged the west end and the entire building is now at risk.

50. On Scott's reputation see Gavin Stamp, 'Introduction', in George Gilbert Scott, *Personal and Professional Recollections*, ed. Gavin Stamp, Stamford, 1995, pp.d-e.

51. For an account of the building of Holy Trinity, Avonside, see Lochhead, *op. cit.* [note 28], pp.201–3; and Chris Cochran, *Holy Trinity, Avonside, Christchurch: Conservation Plan*, Wellington, 2009, pp.3–9.

52. Robert Paul quoted in Skinner, *op. cit.* [note 40], p.252. The tower shown in the lithograph of Avonside Church published in Paul's book was probably never built.

53. The 1876 chancel was not so fortunate, collapsing in the earthquake of 22 February 2011. The entire church has now been demolished.

54. The church was constructed in three stages between 1864 and 1913. See Hardwicke Knight, *Church Building in Otago*, Dunedin, 1993, pp.204–7.

55. For an account of Rumsey's career see Peter Richardson, 'Building the Dominion: Government Architecture in New Zealand, 1840–1922', Ph.D. thesis, 2 vols., University of Canterbury, 1997, vol. 1, pp.153–8. For an entertaining account of his antipodean experiences, see also [Edward Rumsey] 'An Architect in the Antipodes', *Builder*, 30 March 1867, pp.228–9.

56. For an account of the building of St John's Anglican Cathedral, Napier, see Lochhead, *op. cit.* [note 28], pp.162–73.

57. *Ibid.*, pp.173–80.

58. *Church Gazette* quoted in E.A. Evans, 'St Mary's Church, Parnell, Auckland', unpublished report prepared for the New Zealand Historic Places Trust, Wellington, 1975, p.10.

5 · The Introduction of Ecclesiology to Nova Scotia

PETER COFFMAN

By 1867 'the triumph of ecclesiology was incontestable', according to J. Mordaunt Crook, '… a group of Cambridge undergraduates had succeeded in transforming the appearance of every Anglican church in the world'.[1] The architectural evidence of that triumph is unmistakable in towns and cities throughout England and the former British Empire. The very abundance of this evidence, however, can obscure just how vigorously contested that triumph was at the time. Nowhere is this better illustrated than in the colonial diocese of Nova Scotia. While the impact of ecclesiology is vividly affirmed in communities as widespread as Digby, Mahone Bay [fig. 5.2], and Cape Breton, the introduction of its principles to Nova Scotia was met with bitter resistance that was overcome only gradually.

Nova Scotia has the singular distinction of being the first colonial diocese in the history of the Church of England. Founded in 1787, the first bishop was Charles Inglis, a United Empire Loyalist who had spent much of his working life in New York, before anti-British post-revolutionary sentiment caused him to flee back to England.[2] The founding of the new diocese of Nova Scotia was, in large part, intended to provide a social and spiritual bulwark against the evils of dissent, republicanism and revolutionary spirit.[3] A staunch Loyalist, for whom loyalty to the Crown and loyalty to the Established Church were two sides of the same coin, one of Inglis's most enduring legacies was the erection of nearly fifty Anglican churches throughout is huge diocese (which initially included the whole of eastern British North America).[4] St Mary's, Auburn (begun 1790), is a well-preserved example that shows Inglis's preferred form [fig. 5.1]. It is essentially a Gibbsian arrangement in the style of St Martin-in-the-Fields – in other words, a classical building with a tower and spire, and with a galleried interior designed to focus all attention on the pulpit. This architectural paradigm was deeply entrenched in Anglican Nova Scotia by the time of Inglis's death in 1816.

In the same year that the Cambridge Camden Society was founded (1839), the diocese of Newfoundland was separated from Nova Scotia, and the creation of the diocese of New Brunswick followed in 1845. The latter became something of a showcase for the successful adoption of ecclesiological Gothic, thanks to the Tractarian values and architectural expertise of its first bishop, John Medley (1804–92).[5] Medley arrived in his new diocese to find an architectural landscape in the grip of Inglis-inspired Gibbsian classicism with uncomfortable echoes of 'the buildings erected by the Puritans'. These box-like structures, he complained,

Fig 5.1 | St. Mary's Church, Auburn, Nova Scotia [Peter Coffman].

were often without a chancel, and had flat roofs with no exposed timbers. The pulpit was where the altar was supposed to be, and the square pews were auctioned to the highest bidder. In short, Medley concluded that at the time of his arrival there were no examples of 'correct' ecclesiastical architecture in North America, let alone New Brunswick.[6]

As a founding member of the Exeter Diocesan Architectural Society, this was a problem that Medley was uniquely well positioned to solve. In 1841, he had written a pamphlet on Gothic (*Elementary Remarks on Church Architecture*) that had drawn warm praise from the Cambridge Camden Society. That Society held out great hopes for the impact Medley would have on New Brunswick, and he did not disappoint them.

The first new church that Medley completed was St Anne's Chapel in Fredericton, designed by Frank Wills [fig. 5.3]. With this church, Ecclesiology may be said to have truly arrived in British North America. Utterly unlike anything the colony had seen before, it is an impeccable paraphrase of an Early English Gothic parish church. *The Ecclesiologist*, not known for handing out extravagant praise lightly, was unqualified in its enthusiasm:

> ... for the first time, the inhabitants of New Brunswick have ... the
> opportunity of learning what was the intention and true spirit of those
> venerable services which they have inherited from their Mother Church
> of England.[7]

Medley's success at St Anne's was followed by the building of Christ Church Cathedral in Fredericton, begun in 1845 and completed in 1853, also by Frank Wills, with modifications made by William Butterfield.[8] Where St Anne's had been a paraphrase of medieval England, Christ Church used direct, verbatim quotations: most of the church west of the crossing (most unmistakably the west façade) is based on St Mary's Church in Snettisham, Norfolk, while Butterfield's east window is a copy of the east window at Selby Abbey in Yorkshire.

Edward Feild, who arrived in Newfoundland as the second bishop of that diocese in 1844, experienced a somewhat different trajectory from Medley's.[9] Finding his colony numerically dominated by Irish Roman Catholics, Feild struggled to build correct, English Gothic churches in the face of this perceived menace, spurred on by what seemed to be a perpetual state of crisis. His architectural patronage began with his own cathedral in St John's, and spread throughout his diocese (including Labrador) despite an intransigent geography and brutal climate.[10] Feild's cathedral – only the nave of which was completed during his lifetime – was designed by George Gilbert Scott [fig. 5.4]. Mainly Early English in style, it drew praise from *The Ecclesiologist* for its faithful 'Englishness':

> ... the church by its durability and solid size, as well as by its
> unmistakable English and authenticated character, will ... fully and very
> creditably represent our Church in one of the most cheerless of its seats.[11]

While ecclesiological Gothic left its mark on New Brunswick and Nova Scotia

Fig 5.2 | St. James Church (*left*), Mahone Bay, Nova Scotia [Peter Coffman].

from the middle of the 1840s, its progress in Nova Scotia was considerably slower. This is probably explained by two factors: it already had a more deeply entrenched non-Gothic architectural tradition than either of the two newer dioceses, and no bishop with Tractarian leanings appeared to tamper with that tradition until the mid-1860s. The first church in the province to come to the attention of the Ecclesiological Society – and to apparently reflect some of its principles – was a small chapel at Falkland (now Ferguson's Cove), just across the Northwest Arm from Halifax. The church, built in 1846, came to the attention of the Society in 1848:

> *The quarterly paper of the Society for the Propagation of the Gospel in Foreign Parts contains a wood-cut of this new church, which we are very happy to see is really like a church .... We should imagine that the design (which we can hardly judge by the wood-cut) would admit of criticism, but we should not like to criticize such a first attempt.*[12]

Not a trace of the church remains, so, like the ecclesiologists, we are forced to assess the building from the SPG woodcut [fig. 5.5].[13] The reasons for the Society's happiness are clear: the church is clearly Gothic, apparently Decorated, has a well-defined nave, chancel and south porch, steeply pitched roofs and belfry above the west end. The last was in fact an object of criticism, as the ecclesiologists found it 'sadly too lofty' – an undeniable fact if one's point of reference is

Fig 5.3 | St. Anne's Chapel, Fredericton,
New Brunswick [Peter Coffman].

Fig 5.4 | Cathedral of St. John the Baptist,
St. John's, Newfoundland [Peter Coffman].

Fig 5.5 | Church of England Chapel, Falkland, Nova Scotia [SPG Quarterly Report].

Fig 5.6 | Bishop Hibbert Binney [Diocese of Nova Scotia and Prince Edward Island Archives].

medieval models such as St Michael's, Longstanton, Cambridgeshire. However flawed, the chapel at Falkland suggests an awareness of ecclesiology that is not so far removed from that of its exact contemporary, St Anne's Chapel in Fredericton.

As promising a start as this may have seemed, the one church in Nova Scotia that an ecclesiologist could love (or at least approve of) remained a complete anomaly for twenty years. At the time the chapel was built in Falkland, Nova Scotia lacked a champion of ecclesiology in the mould of Medley or Feild – a bishop whose Tractarian views would provide the impetus for a new architecture. That changed in 1851, with the arrival of Hibbert Binney as fourth Bishop of Nova Scotia.

Hibbert Binney (1819–87) was the first Nova Scotian-born bishop of that diocese [fig. 5.6].[14] His local roots (he was born in Sidney, on Cape Breton Island) helped smooth his appointment as bishop, although having left the colony for England at the age of four, his memories of his homeland would have been sketchy at best. He was ordained in Oxford in 1844, and received an MA there in 1844. He was of precisely the right generation to be profoundly influenced by the Oxford Movement, and arrived in Nova Scotia in 1851 with a clear agenda to reform what he would have regarded as the somewhat old-fashioned and deeply entrenched practices of the oldest colonial diocese.

Binney brought three distinct but linked innovations to Nova Scotia. First was the Tractarian liturgy, along with its accompanying alterations in church furniture and clerical vestments. Second was the appropriate architectural setting for this liturgy, which was Gothic. Third was the medieval Synodical form of diocesan administration, in which authority and assets would be centralised.[15] All were rooted in a desire to return to ancient forms of worship that were appropriate to the ancient linage of the Church of England. Like other Tractarians, Binney held that the ultimate source of the authority of the Anglican clergy was the Apostles themselves:

> We believe that our present ministers can trace back their authority, as derived by succession, through an unbroken line, from those who received their commission from Christ; whereas these other bodies cannot pretend to claim any such authority for their ministers.[16]

Tractarianism and Ecclesiology were two sides – liturgical and architectural – of the same coin. Consequently, both were equally vulnerable to the allegation that they were no more than thinly disguised versions of Roman Catholicism. Low-Church, anti-Tractarian periodicals such as *The Record* lost no opportunity to point out the errors of the Cambridge Camden Society:

> ... these young adepts at church architecture are somewhat systematically seeking to aid the Oxford movement in favour of the old superstitions; and in the midst of a great deal of trash there is much also that is really mischievous.[17]

In Newfoundland, Edward Feild had complained that he had been attacked in *The Record* 'for having a regular Tractarian Curate', a charge that 'would alienate I know how many of these ignorant and excited fishmongers from me and the Church'.[18] For Hibbert Binney in Nova Scotia, however, the opposition was of another order of magnitude; not only was it loud, public and hostile, but it came primarily from his own clergy.

That opposition coalesced around the Rev. George William Hill, Rector of St Paul's Church in Halifax. For the Rector of St Paul's to become the bishop's most bitter opponent was unfortunate on several levels. Not only was St Paul's the oldest parish in the diocese, but the church – a Gibbsian building begun in 1750 – had the distinction of being the oldest protestant church in British North America.[19] Because of its venerable status, it also served as the titular cathedral for the Bishop of Nova Scotia; the discomfort associated with the bishop being publicly opposed by the Rector of his cathedral church can be imagined.

The disagreement between Binney and Hill came to a head in 1866. In a bluntly worded letter addressed to his parishioners and published for all to see, Hill complained that, under Binney's stewardship, the Church in Nova Scotia was promoting 'anti-Protestant and unscriptural views' that were 'antagonistic to the doctrines held by the Church of England'. He denounced what he considered to be 'mimicry of the language used by the Church of Rome', and concluded 'that our Church is in peril I have no doubt: all over the world it is being rent asunder, chiefly by the introduction of emblematical novelties'.[20]

While Hill's opposition was not universal among the Nova Scotian clergy, he had an extremely vocal ally in the Rev. James Robertson, Rector of Wilmot. In another letter of 1866, also printed and publicly distributed, Robertson argued vigorously against the synodical system.[21] He admonished Binney with a cautionary tale of a certain gentleman named Ward, who some years earlier had been expelled from Oxford for holding several strange dogmas, among them that the Reformation had been an unfortunate error. 'I hope you do not mean,' Robertson warned Binney, 'to subject yourself to the same measure of reprehension by proposing ... to follow so pernicious an example as the synods of the middle ages.'

Not coincidentally, as this argument was reaching its venomous peak, Binney was making his first significant marks as an architectural patron. Specifically, there were four church projects dating from 1866 that were clear architectural statements of the principles that were proving so controversial among some of his colleagues. Of the four, one was never built, and two of the other three do not survive. But all represent watersheds in the architectural manifestation of Binney's reforms.

St Michael's, Windsor Forks, is the only one of the four extant [fig.s 5.7, 5.8]. Notwithstanding the late twentieth-century re-cladding of both the exterior and interior, the ecclesiological principles are still plainly evident. The separate nave, chancel and porch; the open timber ceiling; the steeply sloping roof; the steps leading to the chancel, the stained glass; the primary position of the altar and subordinate position of the pulpit; all are features that the Society found eminently virtuous. Predictably, Binney's nemesis, the Rev. Hill of St Paul's, was deeply unimpressed by St Michael's. When a report on its consecration appeared in the Church organ, *The Nova Scotia Church Chronicle*, praising all the features listed above, Hill took it as yet more evidence of the Church's dangerous slide into Popery, and vigorously encouraged his flock to refrain from subscribing to the magazine.[22]

Far more architecturally ambitious than St Michael's was the church that Binney never built. In his Charge to the Clergy of 1866, Binney proclaimed the need for a stone cathedral. By then, he had moved his Episcopal seat from St Paul's to St Luke's Church (also in Halifax) – a building that had the twin benefits of being at least superficially Gothic (albeit of the Commissioners' Church variety rather than ecclesiological), and of being some distance from the Rev. George W. Hill. The building's inadequacies, however, were obvious to Binney, and in his 1866 *Charge* he made sure they were to his clergy:

> This building [St Luke's] is not indeed what we would desire, and it is
> little creditable to this Diocese that, although the oldest, it is almost the
> only one of the eight North American Dioceses, in which there is not a
> stone Cathedral, the only one in which when we were honored by the
> presence of the Prince of Wales, there was nothing more than an ordinary
> Parish Church which he could be requested to visit.[23]

Binney would certainly have been aware of the impressive stone cathedrals erected by his brethren in Fredericton and St John's. By comparison, St Luke's [fig. 5.9]

Figs 5.7, 5.8 | St. Michael's Church, Windsor Forks, Nova Scotia [Peter Coffman].

was decidedly lacking in what Beresford Hope termed 'the cathedral character';[24] in fact, it was merely a parish church to which Binney had added a chancel.

Binney's initial attempts to raise money for a new cathedral were unsuccessful, and the project languished for several years. Late in 1872, buoyed by a donation of land from his father-in-law and some conditional cash donations, he launched the fundraising campaign again. In an open letter to all Anglicans in the Diocese of Nova Scotia written at Christmas in 1872, he announced:

> I have procured a design from an eminent English architect for a building to accommodate 900 persons, without galleries. It is very plain and depends for its beauty upon its proportions and its solidity, but it will cost not less than 25,000 to 30,000 Pounds Currency. This is a large sum, but unless we are wholly devoid of the spirit in which King David was animated, the amount ought to be readily obtained.[25]

Unfortunately, Binney does not name the eminent English architect to whom he refers. The earliest existing drawings for the proposed cathedral date from 1888, and are by Arthur Edmund Street.[26] It is tempting to speculate that the design of sixteen years earlier could have been by his illustrious father, George. Given the work of George Gilbert Scott in Newfoundland, and of William Butterfield in New Brunswick, there is ample precedent for the involvement of as eminent an architect as Street in Atlantic Canada. Unfortunately, not a trace of this first design seems to have survived, and speculation it must remain.

In early 1873, *The Halifax Citizen* reported:

> Bishop Binney has revived the subject of building a new Episcopal cathedral in a circular letter, in which he offers to contribute £1000 towards the cost, which is estimated at £25,000 to £30,000. He has already a free grant of the site and something over £10,000 promised, provided the balance can be raised.[27]

Despite this apparently promising start, Binney's Achilles heel remained fundraising. This was not merely a reflection of the comparative poverty of the colony of Nova Scotia. The Roman Catholics were also in search of building funds. Shortly after Binney re-launched his cathedral campaign, *The Halifax Citizen* reported that, 'Ten thousand dollars were subscribed at a meeting in the basement of St Mary's [Roman Catholic] Cathedral on Sunday afternoon, towards finishing the front of the Cathedral.'[28] Binney's problem was not that Anglicans could not raise any money, but that their goals in doing so were not always helpful to him. One month before the Roman Catholic fundraiser, the Anglican parish of St George's – second in age and prestige only to St Paul's among Halifax parishes – was also busily raising funds. But that money ('about six hundred dollars') was not intended to aid the Bishop in his initiatives, but to oppose him – it was to cover legal costs required to fight Binney over a disputed pastoral appointment.[29] It was in this hopelessly inauspicious and frequently hostile environment that Binney re-launched his cathedral campaign.

Binney's last chance to build his cathedral was in 1887, the centenary of the diocese.[30] Although nowhere near enough money was in hand to complete the project, Binney presumably hoped that enthusiasm and momentum from centennial celebrations would be enough to see the project through (or at least get it started). A date was set to lay the cornerstone – 12 August 1887, the centenary of Charles Inglis's consecration.[31] A ceremony was planned, and numerous dignitaries (including Bishop John Medley of Fredericton) were invited. On April 30, just over three months before the day that he had been working toward since 1866, Binney died at the age of sixty-seven. The cornerstone was duly unveiled by Bishop Medley on the appointed date in August, but not another stone of Binney's cathedral was ever laid.[32]

While the failure of Binney's cathedral project may seem predictable in retrospect, in 1866 the possibility of success was (or at least must have seemed) genuine. In addition to church at Windsor Forks discussed above, Binney opened two new churches in Halifax that he clearly regarded as watersheds. In his Pastoral letter of that year, he announced:

> Two new churches have been erected in accordance with the increased
> knowledge and improved taste of our day, very different from any
> specimens to be found within the Diocese when I first arrived here.[33]

Similarly, in his charge to the clergy of that year, Binney boasted of 'two new churches now nearly completed in this city, which show a great advance upon all previous attempts...'[34] Binney again bragged of 'two new churches, one of them being of brick and stone, and holding more than 800', in a letter to the SPG in 1867.[35]

The two new Halifax churches, neither of which survives, were St Mark's and Trinity Church. Both were designed by David Stirling, a Scottish-born and trained architect who had immigrated to British North America (BNA) in 1847.[36] Stirling began a thirteen-year stint in Halifax in 1862, in partnership with fellow Scotsman William Hay, who had arrived in BNA as George Gilbert Scott's clerk of works in St John's.[37] Among Stirling's Halifax apprentices was William Critchlow Harris, who would go on to an extremely productive career as a designer of churches in Nova Scotia and Prince Edward Island.[38] With Hay's return to Scotland in 1865, Stirling was the most knowledgeable and experienced architect of Gothic in Nova Scotia, and thus a natural choice for Binney.

St Mark's Church was consecrated on December 2, 1866 [fig. 5.10]. The photograph reproduced here dates from around 1909, and shows aisles that were added in 1888 (possibly by William Critchlow Harris). The church was opened in December 1866, at a service that was, according to the local press, filled to overflowing, with 'hundreds' turned away.[39] The sermon was preached by Binney, and a collection was taken up to cover the balance of the building costs (estimated at the time to total £1,400).[40] The Gothic forms, steep rooflines, lancets, hoodmoulds and buttresses show a degree of historical literacy that was new to Nova Scotian Gothic, and that reflect the 'increased knowledge and improved taste' of which Binney boasted. The dimensions reflected the clear, simple geometric proportions that Stirling often favoured: the length of the nave was 80ft, the chancel was a square of exactly one quarter that size (20ft), and the vestry and porch were squares of 11ft and 13ft, respectively.[41] The interior seated over 400 beneath a hammer-beam roof. St Mark's perished along with most of its parishioners in the Halifax explosion of 1917.

The other new Stirling church opened by Binney in Halifax that day was the more ambitious Trinity Church. Built in a poor neighbourhood of Halifax, the church announced 'This Church is for the poor and the stranger forever' above the main entrance.[42] Faced externally in brick with a roof of Newfoundland slate, Trinity is a simple but monumental design, with pinnacles, massive corner buttresses and transepts adding to the monumentality.

The Notman Studio photograph of the interior [fig. 5.11] shows a deep chancel, a polygonal apse and an impressive hammer-beam roof. An ecclesiologist would doubtless also praise the placing of the pulpit off to the side of the chancel arch, the Decorated windows and the steps leading up to the chancel (not visible here). The church seated over 800, and reportedly on opening day, 'every seat was occupied'.[43] Trinity Church was demolished in the late twentieth century.

As well as being a breakthrough for Ecclesiology in Nova Scotia, Trinity church is fascinating for putting into particularly sharp focus the tensions that surrounded the introduction of ecclesiology and Tractarianism into Nova Scotia. The rector was J.C. Cochrane, a committed low-churchman who had been at odds with his bishop on a number of occasions. On the day of the church's opening, Cochrane preached a thankful sermon in the presence of his bishop in which he expressed his gratitude for the new building where his congregation was meeting for the first time. Barely one month later, in his New Year's sermon to the parish (this time, not in the presence of his bishop), Cochrane delivered this stern warning to his flock against 'perverse disputings, error and false doctrine':

> Watch against any change in the customs of the Church to which you
> belong ... Watch against any innovations in our form of worship. Regard
> them as the forerunners of unsoundness of doctrine, and departure from
> the faith ... Look out, not for what may attract and please the eye, but what
> may mend the heart and fix your minds on Jesus, and save your souls.[44]

That these words were profoundly at odds with the new architectural setting in which they were preached was likely as obvious to the congregation as it is to the historian.

With such vigorous and vocal opposition, it may seem surprising that Binney managed to get anything built at all. But that same New Year's, other members of his clergy gathered in St Luke's to deliver a message to their bishop. Led by the Dean, William Bullock, they read an address to Binney that began with a declaration of 'profound veneration' for his office and 'much respect' for his person. Bullock continued:

> We have read with astonishment and sorrow the letters recently
> addressed to your lordship, in which grave charges, as to doctrine and

Fig 5.9 | St. Luke's Church, Halifax, Nova Scotia [Diocese of Nova Scotia and Prince Edward Island Archives].

Fig 5.10 | St. Mark's Church, Halifax, Nova Scotia [NSA Photograph Collection: Places: Halifax: Churches: St. Mark's Anglican Church].

Fig 5.11 | Trinity Church, Halifax, Notman Studio, photographer [NSA, Notman Studio Collection, 1983–310 no. 34924].

> *practice, are proferred against you. Of these your Lordship's replies may*
> *well be considered a sufficient refutation.*[45]

This gesture of support was accompanied by a gift of a pastoral staff as a material token of their esteem: 'it will remind us of your episcopal power and authority – it will remind you of our submission, respect and confidence'.[46]

As support grew among his clergy and throughout his diocese, ecclesiology would finally triumph in Nova Scotia. By the time of Binney's death in 1887, *The Daily Examiner* was able to report in is obituary:

Almost every church building has either been enlarged and improved, or a new one built in its place. The old fashioned four-square building, with the great three-decker pulpit, so familiar to the older portion of our readers, has given place to more seemly structures, and in some places to very handsome and ecclesiastical edifices...[47]

It would seem that J. Mordaunt Crook was correct concerning the incontestable triumph of ecclesiology; in the case of Nova Scotia, it just took a couple of decades longer.

ACKNOWLEDGEMENTS

I would like to thank the many people who assisted me with this research, in particular Lorraine Slopek, Diocesan Archivist of Nova Scotia and PEI; Garry Shutlak of the Provincial Archives of Nova Scotia; Claire Campbell and Shirley Tillotson of Dalhousie University; Bill Naftel, Stephen Archibald and Sheila Stephenson of Halifax; and Canon Robert Tuck of Charlottetown. I am also grateful to the Killam Foundation for its extremely generous support for the research project of which this forms a part, and to Alex Bremner for his tireless work in bringing together a diverse international community of scholars united by a common passion.

NOTES

1. J. Mordaunt Crook, *The Dilemma of Style*, London, 1987, p.63.

2. On Charles Inglis, see B. Cuthbertson, *The First Bishop: a Biography of Charles Inglis*, Halifax, 1987.

3. J. Fingard, *The Anglican Design in Loyalist Nova Scotia*, London, 1972.

4. On Inglis's churches, see Cuthbertson, *op. cit.* [note 2], pp.123–35.

5. On Medley and his architectural legacy, see D. Richardson, *Christ Church Cathedral, Fredericton, New Brunswick*, unpublished M.A. thesis, Yale University, 1966; G. Finley, *New Brunswick's Gothic Revival: John Medley and the Aesthetics of Anglican Worship*, unpublished Ph.D. thesis, University of New Brunswick, 1989; G. Finley and L. Wiggington, *On Earth as it Is in Heaven: Gothic Revival Churches of Victorian New Brunswick*, Fredericton, 1995; Peter Coffman, *Newfoundland Gothic*, Montreal, 2008, pp.51–75.

6. *The Ecclesiologist*, vol. 8, 1848, pp.361–63.

7. *The Ecclesiologist*, vol. 8, 1848, p.378.

8. See Finley, *op.cit.* [note 5 (1995)]; Richardson, *op. cit.* [note 5]; Coffman, *op. cit.* [note 5].

9. On Edward Feild, see H.W. Tucker, *Memoir of the Life and Episcopate of Edward Feild, D.D. Bishop of Newfoundland 1844–1876*, London, 1877.

10. See Coffman, *op. cit.* [note 5]; also Peter Coffman, 'St John's Anglican Cathedral and the Beginnings of Ecclesiological Gothic in Newfoundland', *Journal of the Society for the Study of Architecture in Canada*, vol. 31:1, 2006, pp.3–22; Shane O'Dea and Peter Coffman, 'William Grey: "Missionary" of Gothic in Newfoundland', *Journal of the Society for the Study of Architecture in Canada*, vol. 32:1, 2007, pp.39–48.

11. *The Ecclesiologist*, vol. 8, 1848, p.278.

12. *The Ecclesiologist*, vol. 8, 1848, pp.320–1.

13. The general accuracy of the woodcut would seem to be corroborated by a watercolour, made around the time the church was new,

and preserved in the album (now in the collection of Library and Archives Canada) of Lady Falkland, wife of the Lieutenant Governor and the church's patron.

14. V. Glen Kent, 'Hibbert Binney', *Dictionary of Canadian Biography Online*, 1881–1890 (vol. 11).

15. See 'Bishop Binney and the Nova Scotia Diocesan Synod', *The Journal of the Canadian Church Historical Society*, vol. 3:2, 1956, pp.1–12.

16. H. Binney, *A Charge Delivered to the Clergy at the Visitation Held in the Cathedral Church of St Luke, at Halifax, on the 3rd Day of July, 1866, by Hibbert, Lord Bishop of Nova Scotia*, Halifax, 1866, p.32.

17. *The Record*, 9 January 1843.

18. Letters of Bishop Edward Feild to the Reverend William Scott, Diocesan Archives of Eastern Newfoundland and Labrador, 100.43 Box 2, File 4. Letter dated 20 May 1845.

19. On St Paul's, see J.P. McAleer, *A Pictorial History of St Paul's Anglican Church, Halifax, Nova Scotia*, Halifax, 1993.

20. G.W. Hill, 'A Letter to the Parishioners of St Paul's, Halifax', Halifax, 1866.

21. J. Robertson, 'A letter to the Rt Rev Dr Binney, Bishop of Nova Scotia; containing Observations on the Origin of the Synodical Movement, and a Defence of the Position of its Opponents', Halifax, 1866.

22. Hill, *op. cit.* [note 20].

23. Binney, *op. cit.* [note 16].

24. A.J.B. Beresford Hope, *The English Cathedral of the Nineteenth Century*, London, 1861, p.96.

25. H. Binney, 'To the Members of the Church of England in the Diocese of Nova Scotia', Diocesan Archives Of Nova Scotia and PEI, MG 1, series 1, no. 4, vol. 1.

26. See W. Naftel, *The Building of All Saints Cathedral*, Halifax, 2011.

27. *The Halifax Citizen*, 18 January 1873.

28. *The Halifax Citizen*, 22 April 1873.

29. *The Halifax Citizen*, 8 March 1873.

30. Naftel, *op. cit.* [note 26].

31. *Journal of the Twentieth Session of the Diocesan Synod of Nova Scotia*, Halifax, 1888.

32. A cathedral, Gothic in style, was eventually built on another site to the design of the American architect Bertram Goodhue. See Naftel, *op. cit.* [note 26].

33. *A Pastoral Letter, including a Correspondence between the Rev Geo W. Hill and Himself, by Hibbert, Lord Bishop of Nova Scotia*, Halifax, 1866.

34. *A Charge Delivered to the Clergy at the Visitation Held in the Cathedral Church of S. Luke, at Halifax, on the 3rd Day of July, 1866, by Hibbert, Lord Bishop of Nova Scotia*, Halifax, 1866.

35. Binney to SPG, January 29, 1867, Diocesan Archives of Nova Scotia and Prince Edward Island, MG 1 – Bishop's Records, series 1, no. 4, vol. 1.

36. S. Buggey and G.D. Shutlak, 'David Stirling', *Dictionary of Canadian Biography Online*, 1881–1890 (vol. 11).

37. On Hay, see B. Magrill, '"Development" and Ecclesiology in the Outposts of the British Empire: William Hay's Gothic Solutions for Church Building in Tropical Climates (1840–1890)', *Journal of the Society for the Study of Architecture in Canada*, vol. 29:1, 2, 2004, pp.15–26.

38. On Harris, who was the designer of St James' Church in Mahone Bay (figure 1), see R. Tuck, *Gothic Dreams: The Life and Times of a Canadian Architect, William Critchlow Harris, 1854–1913*, Toronto, 1978; see also Tuck, *Gothic Dreams: The Architecture of William Critchlow Harris* (exhibition catalogue), Charlottetown, 1995.

39. *The Halifax Citizen*, 4 December 1866.

40. *Ibid.*

41. *Ibid.*

42. *Ibid.*

43. *The Morning Chronicle*, 3 December 1866.

44. J.C. Cochrane, *A New Year's Address to the Congregation of Trinity Church, Halifax, 1867*, Halifax, 1867.

45. *Nova Scotia Church Chronicle*, vol. 3:1, January, 1867.

46. *Ibid.*

47. 'Bishop Binney', *The Daily Examiner*, 3 May 1887.

Fig 6.1 | Undated portrait of William White (1825–1900).

6 · William White in the Colonies

GILL HUNTER

William White was born in 1825, the third son in a traditional High-Church clerical family – his great-uncle was Gilbert White, author of *A Natural History of Selborne* [fig. 6.1]. His father and grandfathers were all country parsons who shared the agricultural tribulations of their congregations, as well as the pleasures of country pursuits such as hunting and hare coursing. But this quiet Anglicanism was soon to alter, and in 1836, the year Pugin published the first edition of *Contrasts*, change came to the White family of Blakesley, Northamptonshire. A legacy from William Van Mildert, the last Prince-Bishop of Durham, a cousin of William's mother, allowed William's eldest brother, Henry Master White, to enter Winchester College [fig. 6.2].[1] A year earlier a new headmaster had been appointed: George Moberley, a high-church sympathiser and a close friend of John Keble.

In 1839 Henry White matriculated at Balliol, Moberley's *alma mater*, presumably a reflection of the strong influence of his headmaster, but soon transferred to Wykeham's other endowment, New College. Henry White, a brilliant student, was awarded the Johnson Mathematical and Pusey and Ellerton Hebrew Scholarships. He remained as a Fellow and Tutor after his graduation in 1843 and seemed destined for an illustrious academic career. According to his daughter, Henry was 'deeply influenced by contact with the leaders of the Oxford

Fig 6.2 | Undated portrait of Henry Master White (1820–92), William's elder brother.

Fig 6.3 | Nathaniel James Merriman (1809–82), appointed archdeacon of Albany, Grahamstown, in 1848.

Movement'.[2] Inspired perhaps by Pugin's plans for the restoration of Balliol, in 1844 he became a life member of the Oxford Society for Promoting the Study of Gothic Architecture, which later became the Oxford Architectural Society.

Meanwhile, in 1840, at the age of fifteen, William White joined the practice of Daniel Goodman Squirhill, an architect and surveyor in Leamington. He remained there for five years, acquiring, as he later said 'some of the principles of construction, of quantities, and of the supervision of work', but little 'in the way of design or drawing'.[3] In 1845 he moved to London to be an 'improver' in the office of George Gilbert Scott, whose parents lived not far from the White family home in Northamptonshire. It seems likely that William absorbed the principles of the Gothic revival not only through Scott's office, but also through the Oxford connections of his brother, Henry. After only two years with Scott, William left to establish his own practice in Truro, Cornwall, in 1847, joining the Ecclesiological Society a year later.

Henry White's Oxford career was cut short by his decision in 1848 to travel to the Cape of Good Hope for the sake of his health. He may well have been persuaded by another member of the Oxford Architectural Society and fellow-member of New College, Henry Gordon Merriman. Merriman's elder brother, Nathaniel James Merriman [fig. 6.3], vicar of Street, Somerset, had accepted a proposal from Bishop Robert Gray of Cape Town to be archdeacon of Albany, based in Grahamstown. Bishop Gray was 'richly comforted' by the news from Merriman that Mr White, 'a first-class man', would 'come out for five years at his own expense'.[4] Merriman and White sailed from Gravesend in the *Gwalior* in August 1848. During the long journey White taught himself Dutch and on arrival at the Cape in November set about learning the local Xhosa language.

Bishop Gray had intended to appoint Henry as principal of a new grammar school in Grahamstown, but delays in establishing the school kept him in Cape Town. In March 1849 the bishop opened a collegiate school in the outbuildings of his residence, with Henry as acting principal. Quickly realising that more space would soon be required and that 'there are very great advantages in buildings erected for the purpose', Henry asked William 'to turn the matter over in your mind so as to be ready to send plans if I write for them'.[5] Copies of some of Henry's letters to William, preserved in the archives of Bishops College, Cape Town, illustrate the challenges for an architect designing for a very different environment, and the difficulties of building in the Cape at that time, compounded by the slowness of the mail to and from England.

With the financial help of Angela Burdett-Coutts, a site for the college was purchased at Rondebosch, just east of Table Mountain, and about five miles from the centre of Cape Town. Henry promised to send William a rough sketch of his ideas for accommodating forty to fifty boys – a challenging prospect in a country with little stone, poor bricks, expensive timber and high wages for good craftsmen. What Henry envisaged incorporated a dormitory 'with each bed parted off as it is at Radley', the college that William Sewell (a president and later vice-president of the Oxford Architectural Society) and Robert Singleton founded near Oxford in 1847. He was keen that William should visit Radley to see how each boy was afforded sufficient privacy for his morning and evening prayers.

Both Henry and William sent copies of their ideas to Derwent Coleridge, son of the poet, first principal of St Mark's College, Chelsea, that had been established in 1841 as the National Society's first teacher training institution. This demonstrates the brothers' interest in modern methods of teaching, such as those of Fröbel and Pestalozzi, reflected in William's plan to incorporate a covered play area in his original designs for the college. Henry pointed out 'that in this warm climate the rooms must be lofty, for the sake of coolness', and reminded William that here 'the North is the sunny side'. However, Henry liked 'to have the chance of some sun into a room, though the custom seems to prefer South windows'. He also commented pessimistically that '[t]he Colonists cannot yet appreciate Architecture, and my doubts grow stronger whether Architecture is the right end to *begin* with.'

By April 1851 Henry admitted 'the chance of getting an expensive building like the College finished is less than it seemed'. *The Ecclesiologist* reported in 1852 that William White had 'prepared a very large and very satisfactory plan. It embraced a quadrangle, with chapel, hall, school-room, covered play-ground, cloister, and apartments for the officers and members and servants of the institution. We must say, the design was very admirable.' 'Unfortunately,' *The Ecclesiologist* went on to say, 'the Bishop has been compelled to abandon the idea of building anything beyond the very cheapest and simplest possible structure ... Accordingly Mr White has made a second design for two sides of a court of two long ranges of buildings ... without any pretence at architectural beauty – but with good and suitable outline.'[6] The material was brick laid on Yorkshire flagstones, and plastered, under slate roofs [fig. 6.4].

The accommodation comprised a masters' common room, vice-principal's room and prefects' study, with the chapel at the southern end; a dormitory and master's room occupied the first floor, accessed by an external staircase. A 'short high wall' separated this long range from the schoolroom and lobby, above which was a room used as a classroom and boys' library. Problems with the mail caused a delay in the manufacture of the windows in England, and it was later reported that the chapel was always dark because the windows turned out a foot shorter than ordered. The panes of all the lights were divided not with lead, but with intersecting narrow bars of iron, cutting the brilliant light and making the windows very strong. For the chapel Henry planned seats of teak, to his own design, but found it difficult 'to turn a perspective sketch' of a lectern in *Instrumenta Ecclesiastica* 'into working drawings'. Here we see the obvious dilemma of the clergy trying to implement the strictures of the Ecclesiological Society with little or no practical training and no suitably qualified help to hand. As Henry put it to his brother, 'I often wish I had you at my elbow to advise and devise.'

In his last surviving letter to William, dated 20 June 1853, Henry reported that, apart from the windows and painting, the buildings were finished, but with one deviation: 'the – x-x-x-x – work which you suggested in the plaster. Instead of being in the plaster I found that Mr Penketh [the acting architect] had ordered it of Portland cement, to be fastened on by iron clamps. It has to my eye a somewhat hard appearance, but I had not quite the heart to forbid its being put up, after it was all made – and as it is the only bit of extra ornament we have got no-one here will find fault with it unless I point out the error; & then they will not believe that simple scoring the plaster would have looked better'.

In 1849, and doubtless at Henry White's instigation, William had drawn up plans for a wooden church for the diocese of Cape Town [fig. 6.5]. Five years previously Edward Feild, Bishop of Newfoundland, had asked the Oxford Architectural Society for 'practical information' on the design of wooden churches. It was felt that 'a wooden Church may be built which shall be as Gothic in principle as a stone one', as White's design demonstrates.[7] The roofline is continuous, the chancel arch being articulated externally by a small bellcote. Simple iron crosses decorate the gable ends to east and west and over the gabled south-west porch, while the small paired lancet windows are drawn with diamond-panes. The plan shows an ecclesiologically correct interior: the font stands inside the south entrance porch, a screen divides the chancel from the nave, there are choir stalls, sedilia and pulpit, and the altar stands on a footpace within a raised sanctuary. Unfortunately, there is no evidence that White's design was ever built in South Africa.

Grahamstown was established by the British in 1812 as a frontier garrison on the Cape's eastern border. In 1820 British immigrants were encouraged to establish farms, but the unsuitable terrain and constant incursions from the Boers and the Xhosa forced them to retreat to the town. With supplies brought up by ox cart from Port Elizabeth, trades and businesses flourished and the town quickly became the second largest in the colony. In 1853 the Rev. John Armstrong, vicar of Tidenham, Gloucestershire (a founder member of the Exeter Diocesan Architectural Society), was appointed bishop of Grahamstown. Two years earlier Armstrong had commissioned William White to design the House of Mercy, for fallen women, at Bussage, Gloucestershire. Armstrong arrived in Grahamstown in 1854 to find that after some initial adverse reactions to his wearing of the cassock, Nathaniel Merriman's Tractarian Anglicanism had become increasing influential.

The indefatigable Henry White urged Merriman to build an Anglican church on Settler's Hill, where the Roman Catholics, Baptists and Presbyterians already had places of worship. Merriman expressed his 'earnest hope that he [Henry] may come here and act the part of incumbent to it'.[8] Although Henry remained in Cape Town, he obviously passed the commission for the design to his brother. Despite the death of John Armstrong in 1856, it seems likely that he would have endorsed William White's appointment as architect of the new church. At the end of that year White's designs for the Grahamstown church (St Bartholomew's) were exhibited at the Ecclesiological Society. A site was not agreed until March 1857,

Fig 6.4 | Sketch of Bishops College, Cape Town (*c*.1860), showing (*right*) the chapel with dormitory above accessed by an external staircase, and (*left*) the schoolroom [Courtesy of Bishops College].

Fig 6.5 | White's plan and south elevation for a wooden church in the diocese of Cape Town (1849) [B. Weinreb, *Catalogue 14, The Gothic of Gothick*, 1966].

Fig 6.6 | St. Bartholomew's church, Grahamstown (*c*.1870), showing White's original bell-cote and tall vane [Courtesy Albany Museum (History), Grahamstown].

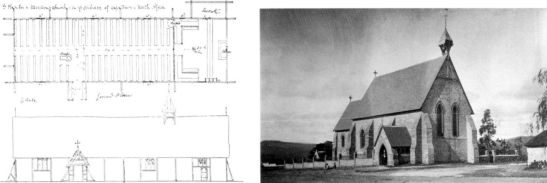

and not formally granted to the bishop of Grahamstown until June of that year.

It was originally envisaged that the whole building would be sent out from England, but the cost of shipping and then transporting all the materials overland must have forced a reappraisal. When the tenders were opened on 30 April 1857 and found to be about £1,100, the building committee rejected them all, as they had already spent about £1,000 on materials, freight and carriage and their own rough estimate for the building was £790. Imported timber was necessary for the framework of the western bellcote, which was similar to the one White had designed in 1853 for the church of St John at Hooe, Plymouth [fig. 6.6]. The wooden bellcote was replaced by a stone tower (not to White's design) in 1893.

White consistently championed colour in buildings: his first communication to be published in *The Ecclesiologist* ('On the Draining and Drying of Churches') concluded with some advice regarding the painting of cast iron gutters which he believed should be painted 'a good deep red, or a good blue … The usual stone colour or lead colour looks very poor when it is first painted, and when it has stood the weather a few months, it looks wretched. Red or blue may appear (to many) rather staring at first, but a few weeks tone it down quite as much as is desirable.'[9] Later designs utilised brick bands to 'warm up' cold stone. At St Bartholomew's, Grahamstown, the moulded bricks for the windows and doors, which would have provided a rich, warm colour (now unfortunately painted pale blue), were shipped from England, and it seems likely that the original quarried glazing would also have been imported. But the stone of the heavily buttressed, aisleless nave and lower chancel is the local Witteberg Quartzite.

When the foundation stone was laid in August 1857, the contractor was listed as a Mr Glass and the superintending architect as a Mr Stitt. However, it was later recorded that the church was built by soldiers, supervised by Merriman and the Rev. John Heavyside, priest in charge of Grahamstown cathedral. Whoever the workmen, they were obviously unskilled, for Heavyside recorded in his diary that he 'twice shewed the workmen how to do the bevel work of string course', and later that he 'Had to take a hammer and trowel … and make them pull out some work'.[10] Although overall it deemed White's design 'thoroughly good', *The Ecclesiologist* of 1857 criticised the east window where the 'interval between the lights and the strange-shaped opening above is too great', but this was presumably to reduce the heat and glare of the sun.[11]

The cost of the church was £2,200, three-quarters of which was donated by Merriman, the first rector, from funds subscribed by his friends in England. Many of these friends were members of the Exeter Diocesan Architectural Society, established in 1841, the first outside the universities, of which, as mentioned, the late John Armstrong was a founder member. 'A Velvet Altar cloth worked by Ladies in England' incorporated many of White's favourite motifs, implying that he was involved in its design. St Bart's (as it is affectionately known) was consecrated by the bishop of Grahamstown in June 1860, although minor works continued for some years as funds allowed.

John Armstrong, the first bishop of Grahamstown, was strongly in favour of colonial integration, stating 'Commonly, the black congregations and the white are quite distinct. The Church has to beat down boldly these walls of partition.'[12] His successor, Henry Cotterill, seems not to have endorsed Armstrong's views, preferring instead to develop separate places of worship for the black and white members of his flock.

At the same time as the grant of land for St Bart's, two plots of land in Fingo, on the north-eastern edge of Grahamstown, were transferred to the bishop 'for ecclesiastical purposes'. Fingo was a settlement where, unusually, the native Mfengu people held the freehold of their land. In 1860 an Anglican mission was established, the first services and school classes being held by the Rev. William Turpin in the open air. In that same year *The Ecclesiologist* praised G.F. Bodley for his design of a church for the diocese, having a 'massive tower' above a chancel 'with round-ended apse', a south aisle and a 'western porch ingeniously contrived so as to exclude the wind'.[13] Aspects of the design can be seen to have evolved from Bodley's earlier churches, such as All Saints', Selsley, Gloucestershire, as Alex Bremner has described.[14] However, as the bishop of Grahamstown was

Fig 6.7 | White's Christ Church, Hatherden (1856–7). The original steeply pitched roof was replaced by a lower one after a disastrous fire caused by a lightning strike in 1976 [Peter Hunter].

Fig 6.8 | St. Philip's, Fingo, Grahamstown (1862–7), from the north-west, showing the western narthex [Peter Hunter].

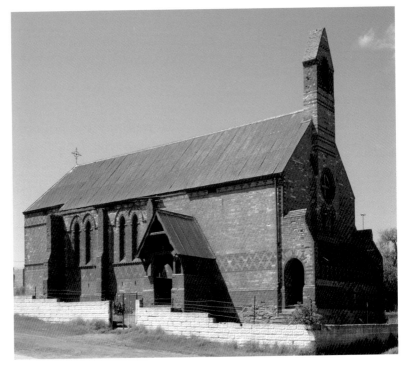

informed by the Rev. Turpin, 'The plainest brick building to accommodate 300 people will ... cost about £600', and 'all the incidental expenses of the Mission are at present borne by the Churchmen of Grahamstown'.[15] Perhaps Bodley's scheme was seen as too ambitious, for the commission seems to have been passed to William White.[16] Perhaps the church in Fingo was White's design for 'a very simple Mission church', which was exhibited at the Royal Academy in 1864.[17]

In 1857 the Rev. John Hardie, who had been curate to White's father-in-law, George Cornish at Kenwyn, Cornwall, was appointed archdeacon of Kaffraria. He may well have been influential in White's gaining the commission. There seems to have been no public comment on the transfer: White and Bodley were close friends from their days together in Scott's office, and from 1859 to 1861 Bodley had shared White's office at 30a Wimpole Street. White had experience of designing 'cheap churches', such as those at Smannell and Hatherden in Hampshire [fig. 6.7]. For St Philip's, Fingo, White employed a similar long, unbroken roofline, canted apse and gabled porch [fig. 6.8]. Elements of Bodley's design were retained, such as the extended chancel buttresses and the western narthex with circular window above, a feature which White later adopted when he rebuilt the west end of the church at Witham Friary, Somerset. The polychrome brickwork of St Philip's is in marked contrast to the sober stonework of St Bart's. The foundation stone was laid in 1864 and the church consecrated three years later, the total cost being £1,580. Merriman was again an ardent fund raiser, and the congregation of St Bart's were generous donors, but Turpin recorded that the Society for the Propagation of the Gospel 'has never given us one farthing towards this Church' despite applications for aid.[18] It became Turpin's ambition to 'make this a strictly African Mission, supplied from African funds alone', and its survival may well be a consequence of that ethos.

White's African commissions continued, with designs for a lectern and credence desk for St Saviour's, Claremont, Cape Town, a font and cover for St John's, Clanwilliam, cheap mission plate exhibited at the 1862 Exhibition, an altar table for the Bishop of Cape Town and, later, the design of a stained glass window for All Saints Memorial Church, King William's Town.

In 1869 the Rev. J. Hopkins Badnall, former vice-principal of Bishops College under Henry White, was appointed rector of Rondebosch, close to the college. The original St Paul's church built in 1834 had been enlarged in 1848–50, possibly to designs by Sophy Gray, wife of the bishop of Cape Town. Further plans for extension of the chancel were abandoned in 1866 on grounds of cost. When Badnall returned to England for his health in 1876, he raised £250 towards a new chancel, and by 1880 White was producing detail drawings. The plans were for north and south transepts, a new chancel, with a large chapel to the south, and a north organ aisle and lean-to vestry [fig. 6.9]. Unlike in Grahamstown twenty-five years earlier, there were now local craftsmen capable of producing the floriated crosses for the gable ends and the complex tracery of the windows. However, costs were high: £8,500, compared with only £4,500 for White's church of St Michael,

Fig 6.9 | St. Paul's, Rondebosch, Cape Town, showing White's chancel, south chapel and northern organ chapel and vestry (1880–4) [Gill Hunter].

Battersea, of the same date. The choir stalls, designed by White, were produced by so-called 'Zon' craftsmen trained at a college established by Bishop Gray in 1858, which later moved out to Zonnebloem, north of Rondebosch. Colour was provided internally by a richly patterned tiled floor to the chancel.

Following the British annexation of the Transvaal in 1877, a new bishopric was created in Pretoria, the former Boer capital. The first bishop was Henry Bousfield, who had previously commissioned White to undertake work at his parish church in Andover, Hampshire. Despite the defeat of the British in the Transvaal in 1881, Bousfield continued to establish his diocese. When he came to England in 1888 to attend the Third Lambeth Conference, he engaged White to draw up plans to extend the simple church of St Alban, Pretoria, to make it more worthy of its cathedral status.

White's design lacks the simplicity of his earlier work in South Africa, with a host of buttresses with pyramidal caps [fig. 6.10]. It was intended to construct the cathedral of the 'indifferent local red brick, specially made, ... thinner and longer ... than usual', with the details made locally using thirty-five special brick moulds sent out from England.[19] A tall spire on the central tower was intended 'when some of the proceeds of the neighbouring gold fields and diamond diggings shall have fallen into the hands of a few faithful and earnest Churchmen'. Bousfield laid the foundation stone in March 1890, and with the few funds available it was intended to build part of the north aisle which would serve as a chancel, with the existing church acting as the nave. However, the constant political and social upheavals, culminating in the wars of 1899–1902, caused the whole scheme to founder until Herbert Baker's design was adopted in 1905.

The 1814 Treaty of Paris recognised the French settlements on the huge island of Madagascar as British, and in exchange for agreeing not to export slaves, the ruler of Madagascar received from the British Governor of Mauritius arms, ammunition and training for his troops. However, with the accession of a new sovereign in 1836, missionaries were expelled and Christianity was banned. In 1868 the new Queen of Madagascar recognised Christianity, and was later baptised. From this time onwards the Bishop of Cape Town was pressing for the appointment of an Anglican bishop in Madagascar. Finally, in February 1874, Robert Kestell Kestell-Cornish, son of the Rev. George James Cornish (a close friend of John Keble), was consecrated bishop. His style was Bishop *in* Madagascar rather than *of* Madagascar, apparently so that the London Missionary Society and other dissenters would not perceive the appointment as a threat. William White had married Ellen Cornish, Robert's sister, in 1855, and had already designed a vicarage and restored the church in Robert's parish of Landkey, Devon.

The importance of the architectural expression of faith in the colonies was emphatically expressed by Bishop Kestell-Cornish. After five years on the island, he returned to England in order to raise at least £5,000 'to build a good stone church, in order that the Malagasy may really see our worship in the fullest power of which it is capable. This has been fully done by the various sections of unhappily divided Christendom who are working in Madagascar … the Jesuits, … Norwegians [and] Independents. We alone, with the *prestige* of representing the Church of England, have hitherto been content to celebrate our worship in temporary buildings, and the natives, not unnaturally, gauge the persistency of our zeal by that which their eyes behold.'[20]

The foundation stone of William White's design for St. Lawrence's cathedral was laid on 13 September 1883. The site was a terrace 25ft above a sacred plain on the eastern edge of the capital, Antananarivo. The design, in stone, is massive to the point of defensiveness, with a windowless apse between transepts redolent

Fig 6.10 | White's design for St. Alban's cathedral, Pretoria (1888–90) [*Church Builder*, 1891].

Fig 6.11 | White's St. Laurence's cathedral, Antananarivo, Madagascar (1879–89), from the south-east [René Lachal].

of watchtowers [fig. 6.11]. Since the French bombarded the city in 1883, this was probably intentional, and its strength has allowed it to survive later vicissitudes. The deeply splayed windows of green tinted quarries filter the strong sunlight, while simple, open-backed benches are eminently suitable for the climate. The baptistery forms the base of the north-west tower and Bishop Kestell-Cornish commented that 'the effect of the font standing in its own octagonal apartment is strikingly beautiful'. A steep flight of sixteen steps emphasises the sacred na- ture of the chancel, while a light iron screen ensures that the altar is visible. Despite the size of the cathedral (140ft x 75ft x 45ft high), the bishop praised 'the perfection of its acoustics'.[21] Consecrated in August 1889, it cost about £8,000, raised entirely by Bishop Kestell-Cornish, mainly from friends in England, but nearly £1,000 from friends in Australia and New Zealand, and £1,000 each from the SPG and the SPCK.

Although there is no evidence that White's plans for a wooden church in Cape Town were ever implemented, it appears that elements of his design were repro- duced in the church at Forteau, Labrador, designed by his brother-in-law, the Rev. William Grey.

A member of the family to which the ill-fated Lady Jane Grey belonged, William Grey, a Wykehamist, read classics at Magdalen Hall, Oxford, graduating in 1842. As well as presenting papers on various architectural topics, in that year he gave a collection of almost a hundred of his architectural drawings and etchings of medieval English buildings to the Oxford Architectural Society, of which he was a member. Ordained deacon in 1843 and priest the following year, Grey accepted a curacy at Allington, a poverty-stricken village of only ninety people, on the

River Bourne near Amesbury, Wiltshire, where he lodged with an old farmer and his wife.[22] Although a convinced ecclesiologist, he was a sensitive restorer: he took down his crumbling church and rebuilt it soundly almost exactly as it had been, prompting the verdict that it 'certainly was as dark, and dull, and cheerless as before'.[23] In 1848 he became secretary and chaplain to Edward Feild, Bishop of Newfoundland, and accompanied him on a visitation to Newfoundland and Bermuda, which was included in his diocese.[24]

Not far from Allington is Abbotts Ann, where, in 1849, the Rev. Francis Henry White, William's father, was living with his wife and five daughters. The youngest, Harriet, aged twenty, married William Grey when he came back to England that summer, and returned with him to Newfoundland. Feild had appointed Grey principal of Queen's (Theological) College, St John's, and diocesan architect. In a letter to the Rev. William Scott, reproduced in *The Ecclesiologist*, Feild had requested 'plain, correct patterns' for wooden churches that he could reproduce with the limited materials and skills available to him.[25] As none was forthcoming, he must have been greatly relieved to have Grey's expertise and experience.

William White maintained his close relationship with his sister and brother-in-law, becoming godfather to the infant William Grey who was born in Newfoundland in 1850. By 1852 Harriet was writing to her brother about their new home at Portugal Cove and in December of that year William Grey described to his brother-in-law the cold appearance of the church which 'is all painted "stone colour" inside which used to be thought the thing, for the inside of churches. I have recommended ochre hereabouts as a great improvement for a wooden building, and besides it is cheaper than the stone colour.'[26] He also suggested in a report to the Oxford Architectural Society that rather than plain, white-painted, horizontal clapboard for houses, if some were nailed on horizontally and some obliquely 'with the frame-work painted with red and the clap board with yellow ochre, the building will have a much more pleasing appearance'.[27] He admitted that the parsonage he had designed for his family at Portugal Cove was constructed in this manner.[28] Love of colour was obviously a mutual concern of the two Williams.[29]

Grey remained a Corresponding Secretary of the Oxford Architectural Society and in a letter dated January 1853 described how the Gothic revival 'can scarcely be said to have begun here'.[30] He also pointed out that most buildings in the colony were constructed of wood, but explained that trees did not grow to any great size, and reminded his readers of 'the sudden changes from frost to thaw, the high winds with furious snow-drifts' with which he had to contend. Grey had given his college students twice-weekly lectures on architecture for 'Here … the Clergy *must* be architects … [I] strongly advise the junior members of the University to qualify themselves for Holy Orders by a practical knowledge of Architecture.'[31] Besides several new churches he had already designed in the colony, Grey planned a new church at Portugal Cove, but returned to England in 1853 for his wife's health before work began.[32]

In 1857 Grey returned to Newfoundland to accompany Feild on a visitation round Newfoundland and Labrador. On the voyage Grey made spirited sketches of the rugged landscape – steep cliffs, deep inlets and scattered settlements.[33] At the head of Forteau Bay on the north-west side of the Straits of Belle Isle, Labrador, Grey recorded Forteau Church, which he had designed and which was consecrated by Bishop Feild on 9 August 1857 [fig. 6.12].[34] The east end of this simple little church appears to have been constructed with some vertical, some horizontal and some oblique clapboarding, as Grey had advocated.[35] But the most obvious feature is the use of diagonal struts exactly as White had shown in his plan for a wooden church in Cape Town of 1849. Described by Shane O'Dea and

Fig 6.12 | William Grey's St. Peter's church, Forteau, Labrador, consecrated 1857 [William Grey, *Sketches of Newfoundland and Labrador*, Ipswich, 1858].

Peter Coffman as 'somewhat like a cross between flying buttresses and tent-pegs', they provided wind-resistance for the stability of a relatively light structure. As Feild had pointed out to the Rev. William Scott (committee member of the Ecclesiological Society), '[t]he frames … are merely placed on a footing of stone, or on piles, and are not otherwise fastened or united with the ground. They are consequently liable to be shaken or moved by the winds, the stroke of which in this country is exceedingly powerful, and require to be stayed and strengthened.'[36] Although this feature does not seem to have been used in any other church designed by Grey, it was obviously effective as the church was still extant in 1902.

The surviving correspondence between William White and William Grey demonstrates their close relationship and mutual interests. It seems that Grey adapted elements of White's earlier design for a wooden church in Cape Town for the similar circumstances in Forteau, where there was a distinct lack of building materials (apart from small timber), a shortage of funds and limited local skills, as well as a difficult climate, including high winds. Perhaps as a result of the success of Grey's church at Forteau, White went on to advocate wood-framing for cheap churches.[37] At St. John's, Littlehampton, Sussex, because it was not on a freehold site, White's design included 'laying the wood sills on a strip of felt without any mortar bed'. Although the six-inch square wood supports of the roof were 'found insufficient to stand the rocking of the wind' and required extra bracing, White did not include diagonal struts to the walls, probably because of the restricted nature of the site.[38]

In 1848 the Rev. William Scott had admitted that he could not understand 'why a wooden window, even of flowing tracery, is utterly inadmissible'.[39] White had long advocated the employment of wood for the construction of churches in England in areas where there was no building stone. His designs for churches at Hatherden and Smannell, near Andover, Hampshire (1856), included wooden windows, because of 'the extreme difficulty of obtaining stone ... and hence also of there being any proper stone cutting masons in the neighbourhood'.[40] Despite White's arguments, the Incorporated Church Building Society insisted that their grant of funds was dependent on the use of stone windows. White managed to compromise with plate traceried heads of stone, but jambs of brick. White went on to design a wooden arcade and clerestory for his cheap school-church, St Luke's, in Park Street, Brighton, in 1875.[41] And a year later, when Canon Erskine Clarke of Battersea required a church to be built quickly and cheaply in the Lavender Hill area of his parish, White designed St Matthew's with tall, wooden arcades.

William White provided some of the earliest interpretations of the Gothic Revival for southern Africa in his designs for Bishops College, Cape Town and his churches in Grahamstown. His cathedral in Madagascar was not only an expression of the power of the Church of England but also of the British domination of this previously French territory. White's colonial experiments in wood also seem to have encouraged him to adopt the material for the speedy construction of low-cost, sometimes temporary, churches in England. His patrons were Oxford-educated Tractarians, committed to the correct expression of worship however remote the location and whatever the limitations caused by climate and lack of materials. Initiated by ecclesiologists, Gothic became an assertion not only of the power of the established church but also of the developing empire.

ACKNOWLEDGEMENTS

I should like to thank Alex Bremner for his guidance and advice in the preparation of this article.

NOTES

1. Declaration of Trust, Northamptonshire Record office: GI/265.
2. MSS Notes, Miss H.M. White, 'Down the Ages' (p.4), Bishops College Archive, Cape Town.
3. *The Builder*, vol. 31, 1885, p.623.
4. Letter to his sister, Anne Williamson, H.L. Farrer, *Life of Robert Gray*, London, 1876, p.183.
5. H.M. White to W. White, 27 April 1849, Bishops College Archive, Cape Town.
6. *The Ecclesiologist*, vol. 13, 1852, p.301.

7. The Rev J.E. Millard, 'On the style of Architecture to be adopted in Colonial Churches', *Oxford Architectural Society Report*, April 1845, p.15.
8. D.H. Varley and H.M. Matthew (eds.), *Cape Journals of Archdeacon N. J. Merriman 1848–1855*, Cape Town, 1957, p.59.
9. *The Ecclesiologist*, vol. 11, 1850, p.155.
10. *Heavyside Diary*, pp.129, 133, Cory Library, Rhodes University, Grahamstown, MS 16 606.
11. *The Ecclesiologist*, vol. 18, 1857, p.65.

12. *Notes from South Africa, made in 1854–5*, quoted in *The Literary Churchman*, II, 1856, pp.168–9.

13. *The Ecclesiologist*, vol. 21, 1860, p.113.

14. Alex Bremner, 'Out of Africa: G.F. Bodley, William White, and the Anglican Mission Church of St Philip, Grahamstown, 1857–67, *Architectural History*, vol. 51, 2008, pp.185–210.

15. Report by the Rev W.H. Turpin, n.d., but with accounts dated Easter 1862, USPG Archive, Rhodes Houes Library, Oxford, D/24c.

16. Bremner, *op. cit.* [note 14], pp.185–210.

17. *The Ecclesiologist*, vol. 25, 1864, p.151.

18. Report by the Rev W.H. Turpin, 30 June 1867, USPG Archive, Rhodes House Library, Oxford, E/21.

19. *Church Builder*, 1895, pp.5–9.

20. *The Guardian*, 3 September 1879, p.1247.

21. *Mission Field*, vol. 36, 1891, pp.14–15.

22. T. Mozley, *Reminiscences Chiefly of Towns, Village and Schools*, London, 1885.

23. *Ibid.*

24. Such visitations were made in the church ship *Hawk*, gifted by the Rev Robert John Eden, rector of Leigh-on-Sea, Essex, later Bishop of Moray and Ross. In 1887 a stained glass window showing the *Hawk*, 'designed and drawn' by William White, was placed in Leigh Church.

25. *Ecclesiologist*, vol. 9, 1849, p.22.

26. W. Grey to W. White, begun 17 December 1852, Dunham Massey Archive, John Rylands Library, Manchester, EGR 5/2/4/45. I am very grateful to Mr John Turnbull for access to material relating to his great-grandfather, the Rev William Grey.

27. W. Grey, 'The Ecclesiology of Newfoundland', *The Ecclesiologist*, vol. 14, 1853, p.160. Perhaps at Grey's instigation, White used oblique boarding in the interiors of many of his buildings.

28. William Grey's sketch, 'Portugal Cove, Newfoundland, The Parsonage and Church' does not show the weatherboarding, William Grey, Collection of Drawings, RIBA Drawings Collection, V & A, SKB/97/2, but it can be seen in a photograph from the collection of Shane O'Dea that appears in Shane O'Dea and Peter Coffman, 'William Grey: "Missionary" of Gothic in Newfoundland', *Journal of the Society for the Study of Architecture in Canada*, vol. 32:1, 2007, p.43.

29. See White's writings on colour, particularly 'A Plea for Polychromy', *Building News*, 18 January 1861, pp.50–55. Grey's love of colour can be seen in his watercolour sketches of stained glass, tiles, wall decoration, etc., William Grey, Collection of Drawings, RIBA Drawings Collection, Victoria and Albert Museum, SKB/93/2.

30. *The Ecclesiologist*, vol. 14, 1853, p.156.

31. *Ibid.*, p.159.

32. Illustrated prospectus by W. Grey, RIBA Drawings Collection, Victoria and Albert Museum, PB 195/3. See also O'Dea and Coffman, *op. cit.* [note 28], p.42.

33. William Grey, *Sketches of Newfoundland and Labrador*, Ipswich, 1858.

34. *Ibid.*, plate 12. Grey's pen and ink sketch of the church from the south can be seen in William Grey, Collection of Drawings, RIBA Drawings Collection, Victoria and Albert Museum, SKB/96/6.

35. A photograph of 1902 from the Diocesan Archives of Eastern Newfoundland and Labrador reproduced in O'Dea and Coffman, *op. cit.* [note 28], p.44, shows similar clapboarding on the south and west elevations of the church.

36. Communication from the Bishop of Newfoundland reported by the Rev William Scott, 'On Wooden Churches', *The Ecclesiologist*, vol. 9, 1849, p.21.

37. William White, 'Cheap Churches', *Building News*, vol. 40, 1881, pp.258–60.

38. *Ibid.*, p.260. Never consecrated, and having been used as a youth club, St John's was demolished in 1967.

39. Scott, *The Ecclesiologist*, vol. 9, 1849, p.20.

40. White to the Incorporated Church Building Society, 8 February 1856, Lambeth Palace Library, ICBS 4953.

41. White, *Building News*, vol. 40, 1881, p.260. 'A more permanent construction was desired' and the arcade was built in stone. The church was superseded by Sir Arthur Blomfield's St Luke's, Queens Park, 1882. I am very grateful to Sue Berry for this information.

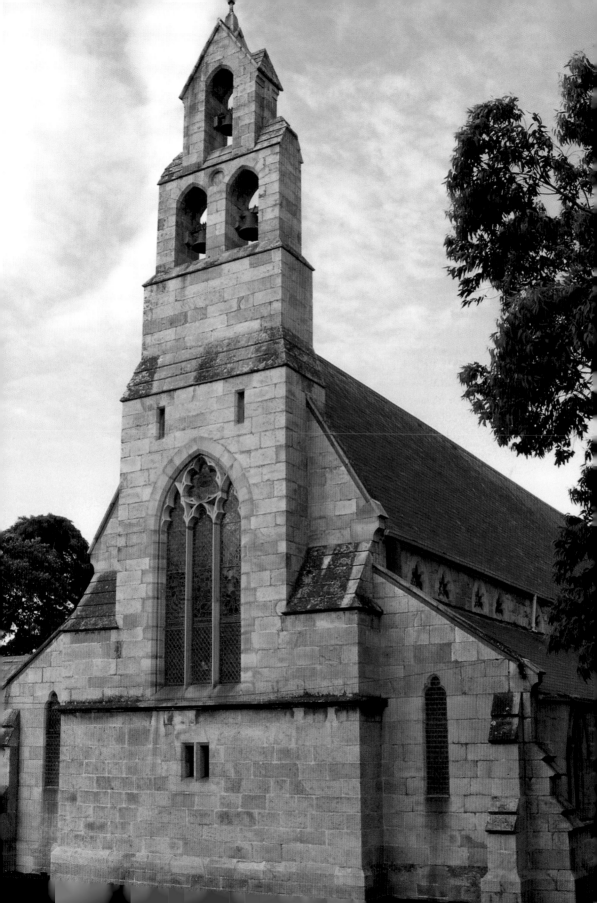

7 · Bishop Robert Gray and Mrs Sophia Gray: Building Anglican Churches in South Africa, 1848–72

DESMOND MARTIN

The drift of English-speaking peoples to the southern tip of Africa had begun slowly after 1806, the year when Britain occupied the Cape for the second time. Following over 150 years of Dutch rule and the formal handover in 1814, the Cape was open to become a productive British colony. In 1819, to address widespread poverty and redundancy of the workforce in Britain, Parliament voted £50,000 'for the passage of carefully selected emigrants to the eastern districts of the Cape Colony'.[1] An article in *The Times* of 18 June 1819 epitomises the stance taken by the upper classes at the time: 'Carry out as settlers all the families who have not bread nor labour here, and we lay for posterity another England, with which ... the mother country will be joined in bands indissoluble.'[2] The unprecedented settler project of 1820 orchestrated by the Colonial Office was to have far-reaching implications in South Africa. Over 4,000 Britons immigrated to the Cape with thousands more following in subsequent years.

In 1839 the Society for the Promotion of Christian Knowledge (SPCK) petitioned the House of Commons to sanction measures to provide 'more effectually for the religious instruction of the Colonies...'. This included the erection of new churches and chapels commensurate with the needs of the colonists. The SPCK added that no new Colonies should be founded without express provision being made for instructing inhabitants 'in the truths ... of Christianity according to the principles of the Church of England'.[3] This petition contributed to the raising of the Colonial Bishoprics' Fund in 1841, to which the SPCK and the Society for the Propagation of the Gospel in Foreign Parts (SPG) gave substantial donations, and the subsequent endowment in 1847 of the See of Cape Town, to which the Rev. Robert Gray was called. During the following twenty-five years, more than fifty new Anglican churches were erected (virtually all in the Cape Colony), statistics that confirmed a remarkable and sustained building boom of the nineteenth century that could largely be attributed to the leadership and energy of one man, Bishop Robert Gray.

HOW THE GRAYS PREPARED FOR BUILDING

Robert Gray was born in Bishopswearmouth, near Sunderland, on 3 October 1809, the seventh son of a Church of England minister. After completing his

Fig 7.1 | St Saviour's Church, Claremont, Cape Town (1850–80) [Alex Bremner].

schooling at Eton in 1826, Robert travelled to the Continent before going up to Oxford in October 1827, graduating BA in 1831 (MA 1834). He then spent a year touring Europe before entering the Church at age 24. In March 1833 he received deacon's Orders in the church of St Margaret, Westminster, and on 11 January 1834 he was ordained priest in Wells Cathedral. Later he was appointed to a living in the parish of Whitworth, close to Durham Cathedral, where he commenced duties on Christmas Day 1834. Thus, from his earliest days Gray was never far from the influence of the Established Church; its churches, cathedrals, church schools and rectories.

It was at Whitworth that Gray met Sophia Myddelton, daughter of Robert Wharton Myddelton. Sophy, as she was better known, and Robert were married on 6 September 1836. They soon became involved in the need for churches in the coal mining villages of Byers Green, Tudhoe and Hillington, actions that may be considered as forerunners to the extensive church-building programmes they initiated in South Africa. The couple had become aware of the support within ecclesiastical circles for the building of churches in the Gothic Revival style; they formulated their approach to architecture through their reading programme and the shrewd observance of church buildings in Britain. In towns and villages, new churches were being built at a faster rate than any other period of the Church's history. Robert had been conditioned by the principles of faith within the Church and had been challenged by the ecclesiastical revival in Oxford in the 1830s that advanced the recognition of the Church 'as the spiritual Body of Christ, and not as a Whitehall Department of State'.[4] Thus, when the call came for Robert to serve in Africa as the continent's first Anglican bishop, he and his wife sailed from England with preconceptions for Anglican liturgy and ecclesiology to a land far removed physically, climatically and culturally from their own.

From the time of his confirmation as Bishop of Cape Town in early 1847, to the time of his departure on 20 December, Gray devoted much of the waiting period to preaching and fundraising around England. Apart from his personal concerns that he would need to raise most of the costs to relocate to Cape Town himself, he prepared for the anticipated building programme. Writing from the vicarage at Stockton-on-Tees on 26 April 1847, Gray prepared a four-page letter of appeal, under the heading *Diocese of the Cape of Good Hope, Provision for Additional Clergy*, which was printed and distributed by the SPG.[5] The letter sketched the extent of Gray's diocese, providing basic demographics and then outlining Gray's three objectives, these being: '[1] to endeavour to increase the number of Clergy who will minister to the members of our own community ... [2] to wipe off the reproach ... for being almost the only communion of Christians that has not attempted to establish Missions ... [3] to erect a Collegiate Institution ... to train young men for the ministry of our Church in the colony'. A fourth objective was implied in the first, as Gray stated, 'I shall also need aid in providing churches, schools and teachers,' ending his letter with a specific request: 'Contributions of Theological books, works on Architecture, Plans, Drawings, etc. of Churches,

Fig 7.2 | St John's Church, Victoria West (1869–74) [Desmond Martin].

Fig 7.3 | St Paul's Church, Rondebosch, Cape Town (1849–75) [Desmond Martin].

Schools or Houses, will be of great use.' The Bishop's readers were left in no doubt that he would be building churches. To emphasise this, Gray also set out statistics of the Church of England at the Cape of Good Hope, which indicated there were a total of only fourteen clergy in the Western and Eastern Cape and ten churches.[6] He concluded by naming the persons who had undertaken to receive donations of books and plans of churches.

At the time, copyright laws did not exist and architects plans and drawings were passed between builders and clients without reference to the originators. Architects contributed to published compendia of styles and details from which interested persons freely copied. On 27 September 1847, Gray was in Cirencester where he recorded, 'Up early, walked to Mr Powell's new church, by Scott – [he] promised me the plans.'[7] It is likely, therefore, that Powell provided him with a plan by Scott (Sir George Gilbert Scott). As the individual church histories reveal, plans by William Butterfield, Henry Woodyer, Henry Jones Underwood and others were held by Sophy Gray. Augmented by working drawings from the Oxford Architectural and Ecclesiological (former Cambridge Camden) societies and possibly other unnamed architects, a most useful portfolio of building plans was compiled before the Grays sailed for Cape Town.

The Grays also appear to have had direct dealings with Butterfield as he later personally supervised the making of windows in England (as well as its nave windows some years later) for St Saviour's Church at Claremont, Cape Town [fig. 7.1]. Butterfield certainly gave Gray a number of specimen plans and drawings,[8] which they used in at least two churches in their programme, these being St Saviour's and St John's at Victoria West [fig. 7.2]. The plan used by Gray for St Paul's Church, Rondebosch, Cape Town, was also possibly one of Butterfield's [fig. 7.3]. On the death of Sophia Gray in 1871, the Bishop approached Butterfield to design the final two bays and a bellcote for St Saviour's as a memorial to his wife. After Gray's own death in 1872, it was Butterfield again who designed the stone memorial to the Bishop that still stands at the top of St George's Mall, Cape Town. It is reasonable to assume that Gray would have known about and endorsed Butterfield's devotion to the High Victorian movement, 'the essence of the Gothic revival'.[9]

BISHOP GRAY'S BUILDING ETHIC: A RATIFICATION OF ECCLESIOLOGY

Bishop Gray disclosed all his sources for church designs in a letter he wrote to the SPG after being in South Africa for only seven months: 'The churches will for the most part be small but they will all be built upon correct Ecclesiastical principles, either from designs published by the Architectural Societies in England, or from plans kindly forwarded to me by Architects in England, who have in this way made many valuable offerings to the Colonial Church...'[10] Confirmation of the above as the sources of the plans used in South Africa is found in Gray's journals, an example being the remark made about St George's Church, Knysna: 'The church is a decorated building (note the window designs) copied from an ancient English church' [fig. 7.4].[11]

To our knowledge, Gray never lectured on church architecture, but he did express his approach to ecclesiology through succinct entries in his journals. Read as a sequence, they reveal his unambiguous mind-set on the building of churches – on what, when, and how he was to build. Because of the nature of public life in Victorian England, the Bishop could make comments on architecture whereas his wife could not. What Sophy Gray believed about this subject is not extensively recorded, but that she thought and felt precisely the same way as her husband is reflected clearly in the churches she designed and in her rare comments made in correspondence.

Probably Robert Gray's first recorded disapproval of a building material is found in his letter to his sister Annie, dated 14 August 1845, two years before the Grays left England. While still in Whitworth, Gray had accepted the Vicarage of Stockton in August 1845 and, although he moved there in September, he made his feelings known to his sister about his 'new' church. He remarked, 'The Roman Catholics have just got a new church by Pugin, and an Independent chapel is now building.' He continues about his Stockton church: 'The church is hideous; brick, round-headed windows, pulpit and desk before the altar, large galleries, pews bought and sold!'[12] This sentence mentions many of Gray's aversions. The church

Fig 7.4 | St George's Church, Knysna
(1849–55) [Alex Bremner].

to which he had been sent was St Thomas in the High Street, Stockton, a rare example in the North East of England of an early eighteenth-century building.[13] Being a Georgian church, it had round-headed windows, was built of brick and had galleries. Thus, Gray was firstly expressing his dislike of the late Renaissance characteristics in this church that included the round-headed windows. He was also revealing his personal disappointment that it was not in the Gothic idiom.

Secondly, as far as Gray was concerned, brick was not the preferred exterior facing. Pugin had in 1841 written, 'A pointed church is the masterpiece of masonry. It is essentially a stone building; its pillars, its arches, its vaults … are all peculiar to stone, and could not be consistently executed in any other material.'[14] The Ecclesiologists also favoured stone.[15] A letter that Bishop Gray wrote to the builder of the church at Colesberg on 24 August 1849 is quoted here as an example of how he expressed his distaste of brick: 'It [the church] would not cost £300 in England even if built of stone. I suppose you must build of brick, though I greatly regret it, for it will never be satisfactory.'[16] The little white-washed church illustrated can still be seen in the small town situated on the national road between Cape Town and Johannesburg.

Thirdly, Gray's remark regarding the placing of the 'pulpit and desk before the altar', shows his disapproval of what was typical of non-conformist churches, where the exposition by a minister of the 'word' from a centrally positioned pulpit (thus taking precedence over the altar) was central to the non-conformist service. By contrast, in an Anglican and Roman Catholic church, nothing should obscure the congregation's view of the altar (the focal point physically and liturgically of the church), least of all the pulpit, which should be set to the left of the altar in front of the chancel arch.

Fourthly, Gray was no doubt aware that galleries were not part of medieval Gothic architecture, so the 'large galleries' in his church at Stockton were ecclesiastically incorrect. During the Gothic Revival the Incorporated Church Building Society did not encourage the building of galleries, though they were permitted with certain provisos.[17] Lastly, in using the disparaging phrase 'pews bought and sold', Gray was referring to the custom of 'pew rents', an abomination to Gray, who believed in the equality of all men before God, entitling them to have equal access to 'sittings' in any church.

Disapproval of another building material is recorded in Gray's first journal covering his 1848 Visitation to the Eastern Cape. During this journey he called at the London Missionary Society (LMS) church at Pacaltsdorp, near George, on 11 September. The church had been built in the Early English style between 1822 and 1825, with Gothic openings and a large battlemented tower at the west end. Gray stated, 'I here found the most church-like looking edifice I have seen in the Colony. It has a tower of very respectable proportions, and is built entirely of stone, and *without a covering of plaster which disfigures every other church I have yet seen* [author's italics].'[18] Gray's strong dislike of plaster, expressed here, was presumably directed at external use only, considering that Pugin had qualified the use of plaster 'for any other purpose than coating [internal] walls ... [as] a mere modern deception, and the trade is not worthy of distinction'.[19] A survey of the Gray churches reveals that of the twenty-two churches with stone exteriors, all but one had plaster over brick internal walls.

The Grays' overarching approach to building churches was to use the Gothic style as advocated by the Ecclesiologists. When the Bishop was in Uitenhage (near Port Elizabeth) in 1848, he wrote on 23 September to the Rev. Ernest Hawkins, Secretary of the SPG, in connection with the progress he had made during his first six months in his diocese with the building of churches. He stated, 'I have been enabled to arrange for the erection of ten additional Churches, the support of six additional clergy. The churches will for the most part be small but they will all be built upon correct Ecclesiastical principles either from designs published by the Architectural Societies in England, or from plans kindly forwarded ... by Architects in England...'[20] The Grays regarded ecclesiastical principles to be synonymous with ecclesiologically correct architecture. Gothic is implied. In stating in his letter that he had 'been enabled', Gray omits mentioning to Hawkins his wife's role as the designer of most of the churches. Gray recorded elsewhere, however, that 'Sophie is architect to the diocese'.[21] It may be surmised that telling the SPG that the design of the new churches in South Africa was being undertaken by a woman would have been considered imprudent for the Bishop, given the reluctance within Victorian society of women to be involved in professions, least of all in those monopolised by men. The individual church histories, however, cite numerous occasions after 1848 when the Bishop was not hesitant to name his wife as author of plans and his adviser in matters architectural.

Further evidence of the Grays' approach being influenced by the Ecclesiologists is the letter that the Bishop wrote to the church building committee in Bloemfontein regarding the plans they had submitted.[22] Gray had suggested that their rector, the Rev. W.A. Steabler, a member of the Camden Society, could easily point out details that were 'incorrect'. In addition, when St Mark's Church, George, was built in 1849, plans of St Mary's, Littlemore, near Oxford (1835), were used [fig. 7.5]. These had been drawn by Henry Underwood and issued by the Oxford Architectural Society in 1840. Working drawings of a number of churches were advertised for purchase by the public in Thomas Rickman's *An attempt to discriminate the Styles of Architecture in England* and J.H. Parker's *Introduction to Gothic Architecture*. Sophy Gray clearly had copies of Underwood's design, as St Mark's is almost an exact copy of Littlemore [fig. 7.6].[23]

Two months after writing his letter to Hawkins, Bishop Gray declared that the labour of building a church was clearly a divine commission that set itself apart from the building of any other structure for secular use. This was apparent in sermons preached in Graaff-Reinet, Eastern Cape, when Gray conducted services in the Dutch Reformed church in the morning and evening of Sunday 19 November 1848. The evening sermon dealt with 'the spirit in which we should enter upon the erection of the House of God'.[24]

PLATE 1.

LITTLEMORE CHURCH.

FROM THE SOUTH EAST.

Fig 7.5 | St Mark's Church, George (1849–50). The crossing and transepts were added in the 1920s to designs by Herbert Baker [Alex Bremner].

Fig 7.6 | Henry Underwood's design for Littlemore Church, near Oxford (1835), as published by the Oxford Architectural Society in 1840.

The spiritual exercise of erecting sacred buildings mentioned here may be coupled with the need for perseverance. In a journal entry made in Grahamstown on 14 September 1850, Gray expressed his grave concerns for the continuance of building projects. Having taken a decision to establish a church, in any one of the many instances, Gray's quandary was how to *sustain* the efforts of the parishioners to continue until the church was complete. He wrote: 'My time has been chiefly occupied in some very anxious business connected with several parishes, arising chiefly from *the difficulty the people find in completing the churches which they have begun* [author's italics]. The expense of building in this colony is greater than any of us have been willing to believe. Though the designs of the churches have all been very simple, they have in most cases exceeded the means which are at the disposal of the several committees.'[25]

It should be remembered in defence of the possible apathy of some church communities, that life in the Eastern Cape for European settlers was far from easy. The Seventh Frontier War (1846–47) had preceded Gray's arrival and the Eighth Frontier War had raged between 1850 and 1853. Gray's answer to these hard-pressed churches was to make frequent visitations to counsel and encourage communities personally, as is evidenced by the fact that during his twenty-five years' of service, he and his wife made twenty-four visitations to towns and villages in his vast diocese that even included the islands of St Helena and Tristan D'Acunha.

Maintenance of building standards was yet another concern expressed by Gray during the 1850 Visitation. While he was in George for the consecration of St Mark's, he recorded on 3 December some of the problems hampering the achievement of high standards and correct styles that he desired for himself and the Church of England: 'Considering the poverty of our people, the inferiority of coloured workmen, and the scarcity of good stone, this church is, I think, a credit to the diocese. It is delightful to see our old English churches repeated in this land. I am glad to find that it is generally admired and appreciated; for this encourages me to persevere in my efforts to get correct churches built.'[26] The thought that a vernacular style of church building for South Africa could have been more appropriate for the new diocese was, on the evidence of the churches built by the Grays, never a consideration. The Grays saw 'old English churches' as a universal style for the Church of England, wherever it was planted. Gray's journal entry continues with castigation of the South African church builder who appeared to be satisfied with mediocrity: 'It requires, indeed, much patience to combat the prejudices, and to endeavour to elevate the tastes of church builders in South Africa. Very many have not a conception beyond the ordinary shapeless brick building, plastered and whitewashed.' The Bishop's personal commitment to sound building practice and correct architectural style is apparent: 'I am happy to say, no incorrect building has been commenced, though the inferiority of our materials and workmanship would make one shrink from seeing them subjected to a very critical eye.'[27]

Comments made by Sophy Gray were understandably more concerned with practical issues than principles. There are a number of instances quoted in the individual church histories where she reveals her firm grip on construction costs and her uncompromising approach to contractors who may have been inclined to exploit church communities. For example, in a letter dated 27 December 1849 to the church leader at Caledon [fig. 7.7], she cited the costs of churches at Port Beaufort (£300), Swellendam (£500), George (£1,000), and Graaff-Reinet (£1,500) to point out the error in the builder's estimates for the Caledon church which, 'do not appear ... to be worth much. He has quite mistaken the character of the building.'[28] In another letter, dated 4 September 1851, she wrote on behalf of the Bishop to Mr Harries, the Churchwarden at St Paul's, Port Elizabeth, in connection with containing the cost of the overall building project. She agreed that the expensive parts of the church should in some way be reduced. A means to lessen the expense was to make the windows in timber instead of stone. In short she believed that the 'change of style from Decorated to Early English would probably make a certain reduction.'[29] Her apparent preoccupation with the architecture of the church buildings did not blind her, however, to the relationship of a church to its setting. She reveals in a letter dated 18 June 1855 that she was aware that her church at Worcester (near Cape Town) needed to relate to its environment and to the immediate streetscape. In submitting revised plans to the minister, she stated: 'I have made the West end and Bell Turret a little more imposing, which

Fig 7.7 | Holy Trinity Church, Caledon (1850–4) [Alex Bremner].

Fig 7.8 | St James the Great Church, Worcester (1852–9) [Desmond Martin].

Fig 7.9 | St John the Baptist Church, Schoonberg (1853–4) [Desmond Martin].

appeared necessary on account of the very large open space [Market Square] and more lofty buildings around it.' [fig. 7.8]

Bishop Gray, in keeping with the Ecclesiologists, held that the building of churches, in particular their internal spaces, had a vital role to play in generating reverence and awe of God. This set church buildings apart from secular structures, just as the 'call to build' a church, mentioned by Gray in his sermon at Graaff-Reinet in 1848, was a divine commission. Of all Gray's beliefs related to Ecclesiology, this is the vital conviction that surpassed them all. Between 11 and 15 October 1855, the Grays visited and consecrated the remotely situated Schoonberg church, St John-in-the-Wilderness, built on a farm in the mountains above George [fig. 7.9]. Gray was well pleased with its Early English architectural style 'very neatly and correctly fitted up'. He wrote, 'I am sure we do not overestimate the importance of real Churches built after the fashion of our English churches. They are creative of reverence and devotion and I have seen enough in this land of the effects of *slovenly and dirty* buildings upon the converts, to make me anxious to guard against such evils.'[30]

In September 1857 an article appeared in the *South African Church Magazine* that appears to have been based on the 1855 journal entry of Bishop Gray, when the Grays visited Schoonberg.[31] The article refers to the painted glass installed at Schoonberg and the arrival of 'stone-work for arches and windows ... prepared under the superintendence of Mr Butterfield ... ' for St Saviour's, Claremont. The

Rev. W. Newman, editor of the magazine, was probably also the author of the article in which, referring to the glass and stone-work, it was said: 'They are signs of a growing love and veneration for the houses of God in the land ... good must indirectly follow ... to society generally, from the introduction of a higher order of art and workmanship into so many buildings throughout the colony.'[32] Newman's article, which may be assumed to have carried the acquiescence of his bishop, concluded with a tirade against 'miserable' buildings: 'Slovenly [a word Gray used in his journal], deceitful, pretentious, vulgar work will make a poor-spirited, careless, thoughtless, dishonest workman.' All who contributed to honest, good work were regarded as benefactors of society and were doing something 'to elevate both those who carry it out, and those who look at it'. Over a year later, a brief but significant statement appeared in the *South African Church Magazine*: 'A Building dedicated to God should not only be a church, but seem a church. The outward and visible aspect should correspond with the inward and invisible life.'[33] It must be assumed that this principle was also endorsed by the Bishop, as the concept is straight out of Pugin's *True Principles*: 'The external and internal appearance of an edifice should be illustrative of, and in accordance with, the purpose for which it is destined.'[34]

Gray's approach to providing places of worship was that one building should suffice for all colours and kinds of people. Separate churches in a town on the basis of colour was indefensible. Between March and June 1869, the Gray's undertook a visitation to the Eastern Frontier that was well documented in three issues of *The Mission Field*. On 30 May the Grays were in Swellendam where the Bishop preached in the morning to only twenty English communicants, presumably at Christ Church, completed in 1855. In the afternoon Gray held an English confirmation with Evensong at which there were fourteen confirmation candidates. In the evening he confirmed 'at a Dutch service, eighty-two coloured people. This is the first confirmation since the coloured congregation, formerly in connexion with the Wesleyans, came over in a body with their teacher to the Church. The little church was crammed. It is only built for 150, but 240 were present... Unhappily, *we have not, as yet, a chapel for these people.* They worship at present in a temporary building ... because there were not sufficient funds to complete the chapel.' The chapel to which Gray was referring was St Luke's Mission Church, which, though started in 1865, was only completed in 1874 [fig. 7.10]. Gray explains why the second church was being built: 'I told our people... *that the difference of language alone justifies our worshipping in separate buildings* [author's italics]; that it is against the spirit of Christianity, and an evil as regards the social condition of the country, to have one church for the black man, another for the white; that as we have but one faith, ... one God and Father of us all, so, where it is possible, we should worship together as one household of faith, in one church, in each place.'[35]

In the previous paragraph, mention is made for the first time of chapels. In considering the Grays' approach to building churches, the word 'church' is used

Fig 7.10 | St Luke's Mission Church, Swellendam (*c.*1865–74) [Alex Bremner].

as meaning a building for public Christian worship. In smaller, poorer communities, where there was a need for public worship as well as for a school, the Grays' practice was to build school chapels, where the same basic space was used at different times for church and school. The school chapel, generally smaller and plainer than the average church, did not have buttresses at the gable ends of the building. Fenestration was usually casement windows to ensure adequate lighting for the chapel's educational function. However, it was not the Bishop's policy to consecrate any building while it had a dual function. In October 1864, when he was at St Helena Bay (near Cape Town), he remarked about the church that had been built, 'At present we use it for a school also, and therefore I do not now consecrate it.'

Notwithstanding all the training, influence and counsel that Gray received for his mammoth building project in Africa, he was not ashamed to admit to his fallibility and indecision, and ultimately his reliance on divine guidance to make decisions. A journal entry made while visiting Prince Albert (a small village near Beaufort West) in 1855 reveals his quandary: 'Lord what would thou have me to do? What ought we to do here? Is it God's will considering the vast field lying open before us? The narrowness of our means, the poverty of our labourers, that we should endeavour to plant our Church here? … and if so, when? Should we do it now, or wait till the English population is increased?'[36]

Despite total commitment to the architectural standards set by the Ecclesiologists and Gothic apologists of the time, it is ironic that when Gray and his family arrived in Cape Town on Sunday, 20 February 1848, they attended the evening service in an early nineteenth-century Greek Revival church, St George's. The Bishop's Letters Patent declared it was to be called a cathedral. St George's was a close copy of Henry Inwood's St Pancras Church, London (1819–22), and had been completed some fourteen years earlier in 1834. The style of St George's did not allow for a chancel as Gray would have wished, its altar was a mahogany table covered with a velvet cloth, there were two galleries, the pews were very high and much of the furniture was not to his liking. Gray declared his disapproval of his cathedral in a letter dated 8 April 1848 to his brother-in-law, Dr Williamson: 'It is as yet doubtful whether I shall have to try and build a Cathedral. Anyhow we must have a new Church in Cape Town; and I should like to throw overboard the present Cathedral, but I must not hurt people's feelings. We shall have a great deal of building and I am sure I don't know from whence the funds are to come.' St George's was to serve as cathedral throughout Robert Gray's twenty-five years as Bishop of Cape Town. Indeed, it continued as Cape Town's cathedral until demolished in 1950 to make way for the completion of Herbert Baker's design, begun in 1901, and still unfinished. Considering Gray's fervent feelings for the Gothic style, it is to his credit that he set aside his personal agenda in favour of the building needs of the Diocese. Over forty churches still stand today as testimony to the sound principles of the building programme implemented by Robert and Sophy Gray.

NOTES

1. A.T. Wirgman, *The English Church in South Africa*, London, 1895, p.75.

2. Quoted in L. Bryer and K.S. Hunt, *The 1820 Settlers*, Cape Town, 1984, p.15.

3. J.A. Hewitt, *Sketches of English Church History*, Cape Town, 1887, p.78.

4. H. Davies, *Great South African Christians*, Oxford, 1951, p.51.

5. USPG Archives, SA Library, Cape Town: MSE 9, pp.427–30.

6. The ten churches were at Cape Town (two), Rondebosch, Wynberg, Simon's Town, Grahamstown, Fort Beaufort, Sidbury, Bathurst, Algoa Bay (Port Elizabeth).

7. C. Gray, *Life of Robert Gray,* 2 vols., London, 1876, vol.1, p.131.

8. The Lady Grey Infant School, built at Bishop Gray's request in 1856, stood on the site of the present Houses of Parliament, Government Avenue, Cape Town. Butterfield had been asked to send plans and the school was built accordingly. It was demolished *c*.1875 when the Parliament buildings were begun.

9. Michael Hall, 'How the tide turned for Gothic Revival Churches', *Studies in Victorian architecture and design,* vol. 2 (2010), p.50.

10. Letter dated 23 September 1848, USPG Archives MSE 9, SA Library.

11. Gray's Journal (*A Journal of the Bishop's Visitation Tour through the Cape Colony in 1850*), London, 1851, p.184.

12. Gray, *op. cit.* [note 7], p.85.

13. J.E. Ruscoe, *The Churches of the Diocese of Durham,* Durham, 1994, p.128. Ruscoe says of St Thomas's Church: 'Tradition unreliably claims Christopher Wren as the architect'.

14. A.W.N. Pugin, *The True Principles of Pointed or Christian Architecture*, London, 1853, p.2.

15. *The Ecclesiologist*, vol. 1 (1842), p.153. Quoting the Incorporated Building Society's instructions about walls: 'To be solidly constructed of stone; or of brick, where no good stone can be procured without great additional expense.'

16. Letterbook, *Chronicles of the Diocese of Cape Town, 1847–1871,* vol.1, p.83.

17. The Instructions stated that the Society 'will not sanction any plan involving the erection of a gallery, unless … it is distinctly shown *that* no room

is unnecessarily sacrificed … on the floor'. *The Ecclesiologist,* July 1842, p.156.

18. Grays Journal (*A Journal of the Bishop's Visitation Tour through the Cape Colony in 1848*), London, 1849, p.14.

19. Pugin, *op. cit.* [note 14], p.2.

20. Letter dated 23 September 1848, USPG Archives, SA Library, Cape Town: MSE 9.

21. A. Hamilton Baynes, *Handbooks of English Church Expansion – South Africa,* London, 1908, p.42. Baynes stated that Bishop Gray described his wife in this way but did not disclose the precise reference.

22. Letter dated 27 August 1850, Church of the Province of South Africa (CPSA Archives, Johannesburg): File AB 1162/A1.

23. *The Ecclesiologist,* vol. 1 (1841), p.10. The editors defend the idea that to be 'churchlike' a church will be expensive to build and state that the 'most churchlike of modern churches, Littlemore, near Oxford, was also one that cost as little as any'.

24. Gray, *op. cit.* [note 18], p.61.

25. Gray, *op. cit.* [note 11], p.139. The committees Gray refers to are the Building Committees that were set up at virtually all churches under construction

26. *Ibid.*, p.189.

27. *Ibid.*

28. Letterbook, *op. cit.* [note 16], pp.131–2.

29. Letterbook, *Chronicles of the Diocese of Cape Town, 1847–1871*, vol. 2, pp.192–3.

30. Gray's Journal (*A Journal of the Bishop's Visitation Tour through the Cape Colony in 1855*), London, 1856, p.66.

31. *The South African Church Magazine*, September. 1857, p.335. This journal was first published in 1850 under the editorship of the first Dean of St George's Cathedral, Cape Town, the Very Rev W.A. Newman.

32. Newman appears to have been the spokesman for the Diocese on matters architectural.

33. *The South African Church Magazine*, February 1859, p.61.

34. Pugin, *op. cit.* [note 14], p.35. Though the Grays had read Pugin there are no references to him or his architectural work in Gray's journals or correspondence.

35. *The Mission Field,* December 1869, p.358.

36. Gray, *op. cit.* [note 30], p.93.

8 · Henry Conybeare and the Gothic Revival in Bombay c.1840–1900

MARIAM DOSSAL

Bombay's signature style of architecture in the second half of the nineteenth century was Gothic Revival. More buildings using local stone were built in Bombay on neo-Gothic architectural principles than almost any other city in the British Empire. Statements of power and religiosity in stone, they reflected an assertive imperial order.[1]

The development of the Gothic Revival style in Bombay is best seen as a continuum. Its beginnings may be traced to drawings submitted in 1847 for the Church of St John the Evangelist, by Welsh hydraulic engineer and amateur architect, Henry Conybeare, (1823–84) a committed Ecclesiologist.[2]

The mature middle phase of the neo-Gothic architectural style in Bombay is represented by buildings designed for 'Frere Town', Bombay's new central business district built in the 1860s and 1870s. Henry Edward Bartle Frere, Governor of Bombay (1862–7), and renowned architect George Gilbert Scott (1811–78), were prominent ecclesiologists who strongly advocated Gothic architecture as the most appropriate style for public buildings. For them and their fellow ecclesiologists, 'Gothic' was the most 'pure' and 'Christian' of architectural styles, suited to promote the spirit of the age, both in Britain and her colonies.

British architects who designed public buildings for Bombay in the second half of the nineteenth century included William Emerson, William Burges, James Trubshawe, Henry St Clair Wilkins, George Twigge Molecey and Walter Paris. They drew on English, French and Venetian Gothic design principles. Even as they did so, the Gothic Revival in Bombay acquired a different character, adapting itself to different climatic conditions and the availability of construction materials. Between the principles and the ground realities of the Indian landscape, there were gaps which had to be filled in by imaginative modifications. Thus, features of Indian architecture were also incorporated and resulted in what may be termed an 'Anglo-Indian Gothic' building style. Architectural historian Christopher London terms this dominant style 'Bombay Gothic'.[3]

Bombay Gothic reached its pinnacle at the end of the nineteenth century with the impressive repertoire of buildings designed by city-based architect, Fredrick William Stevens (1847–1900) and his firm Stevens and Sons. The most notable of Stevens' creations were the Royal Alfred Sailors' Home (1876), the Victoria Terminus, headquarters of the Great Indian Peninsula Railway Company (1888)

Fig 8.1 | The upper loggia of the Library at the University of Bombay (begun 1868), by George Gilbert Scott, George Twigge-Molecey and others. The building was composed in an Italianate Gothic style in reference to the climate. The Clock Tower (Fig 8.3) took nine years to complete [Mariam Dossal].

[fig. 8.2], the Municipal Corporation Buildings (1893) [fig. 8.3], and the Bombay Baroda and Central India Railway Headquarters (1899). Other noteworthy structures in this *genre* included the High Court (1871–9) by Lieutenant-Colonel John Fuller [fig. 8.4]. However, with Stevens' death in 1900 the Gothic Revival period in Bombay came to a close.[4]

The early years of the twentieth century saw public buildings in Bombay built in the Indo-Saracenic style. Prominent among them were the General Post Office (1909), the Prince of Wales Museum (1908–1914), the Gateway of India (1924) and the Institute of Science (1920). Indo-Saracenic drew on Indian and other Eastern architectural traditions, but did not gain ascendancy to become the city's defining architectural style. Indo-Saracenic would in turn give way to Modernism and Art Deco architecture in the 1930s and 1940s; responses to growing nationalist sentiment and a changing political order. Each age expressed its spirit in brick, stone, wood, concrete, glass and steel. Gothic Revival architecture reflected religiosity and imperial might more clearly than any other.[5]

EARLY HISTORY OF THE AFGHAN CHURCH

The Church of St John the Evangelist, also known as the Afghan Memorial Church, was built at Colaba to commemorate the large numbers of officers and soldiers of the Bombay Army who died during the East India Company's expeditions to Sind and in the 1st and 2nd Afghan Wars fought between *c.*1838 and 1843 [fig. 8.5].[6]

Colaba island, the southern-most of the seven islets of Bombay, had served as the military cantonment for the British since Bombay had been received in dowry by King Charles II on his marriage to the Portuguese princess Catharine of Braganza in June 1661. A chapel was built in 1816 to provide Anglican service for the officers and garrison stationed there. It remained a modest place of worship. Henry Moses, a resident of Bombay in the 1840s, noted: 'adjoining the parade ground is a neat little thatched chapel where the English service is performed, but all who wish to avail themselves must bring their own chairs as it does not contain any seats.'[7]

The expansion of Bombay Presidency after the East India Company's victories in the Third Anglo-Maratha war (1818–19), the growing importance of Bombay town and an increase in its military personnel, led to frequent demands for a larger church at Colaba. Designs for a new and large church were submitted by Lieut Col Cowper in the 1820s. The authorities admitted that the drawings were 'elegant', but the estimated cost of Rs 74,012/ – was considered too expensive and plans for a new church were shelved. Renovations were carried out on the existing structure, then referred to as the 'Garrison Church' or the 'Bride's Church', on account of the many marriages of officers and soldiers solemnised there.

In 1843 the need for a large church was reiterated, one which would commemorate the heroic deeds of the many soldiers who had lost their lives in the Afghan Wars and the British expedition in Sind. A memorial church committee was formed early that year. The Rev. George Pigott, secretary to the committee,

Fig 8.2 | Victoria Terminus, Great Indian Peninsula Railway Company (1878–88), by Fredrick William Stevens [Farooq Issa, *Phillips Images,* Mumbai].

Fig 8.3 | Bombay Municipal Corporation Building (1889–93), by Fredrick William Stevens. The building is an amalgam of Indian and Italian Gothic features and style [Farooq Issa, *Phillips Images*, Mumbai].

Fig 8.4 | High Court of Bombay (1871–8) by Lieutenant-Colonel J. A. Fuller. The Clock Tower of the University of Bombay by George Gilbert Scott, George Twigge-Molecey and others, can be seen in the background to the right [Farooq Issa, *Phillips Images*, Mumbai].

urged the Bombay Government in his letter of 27 March 1843, to sanction funds for a memorial church to honour 'those gallant men, who, many of them (had been) deprived of the rites of Christian burial'. The Bombay Government agreed and the church proposals were forwarded to the Court of Directors in London. The Rev. Carr, Bishop of Bombay, emphasised the need for funds, trusting that 'the want at Colaba will shortly be supplied'.[8]

Having received the Court's approval, land adjacent to the Garrison Church was made available for the construction of the Afghan Memorial Church. Concerns over defence required that no buildings be built close to the church, and its steeple was to be constructed tall enough to serve as a landmark for ships and guide them into Bombay harbour.[9]

A MOST 'PURE' AND 'CHRISTIAN' ARCHITECTURE

The early decades of the nineteenth century witnessed fervent religious revivalism in Britain and some countries in Europe. In large part this was a response to political and social upheavals caused by the French Revolution and Napoleonic wars. Rapid industrialisation and unchecked urbanisation added to widespread discontent. Churches offered comfort and thousands flocked to them to hear the word of the Lord. Methodism, other forms of Protestantism, as well as Roman Catholicism, were part of this growing religious sentiment. With it grew a demand for new churches and the restoration of the old. The influential Church Building Act of 1818 prescribed Gothic to be the most 'pure' and 'Christian' of architectural styles. More than 550 of the 620 new churches built in the following two decades were constructed in this style.[10]

Following the Oxford Movement in the 1830s, organisations such as the Cambridge Camden Society (est. 1839) strongly advocated Gothic Revival architecture. The Camden Society began publishing its influential journal *The Ecclesiologist* in 1841, and from 1845 was referred to as the Ecclesiological Society. Through this journal, members of the Ecclesiological Society took it upon themselves to advocate the cause of 'correct' Christian architecture. Renowned architect George Gilbert Scott was an active member of the Ecclesiological Society and, like many of his peers, deeply influenced by the work and writings of A.W.N. Pugin.

It was Pugin, of course, who asserted that only when the piety and public spirit of the Middle Ages was re-established in nineteenth-century Europe would true Christian architecture be possible. Without deep religious sentiment, the built form was but a shell and of little consequence.[11]

Keen that plans for the Church of St John the Evangelist at Colaba be in the Gothic Revival style, applications for architectural drawings were made to the Oxford Architectural Society. When these were prepared by architect J. M. Derick and received in Bombay in 1845, they were considered too expensive to build. Determined not to let the matter rest, Secretary Bartle Frere, then on furlough in England, sought out plans for the memorial church from George Gilbert Scott. On Frere's return to Bombay in 1847 he carried Scott's drawings with him, to hasten the building of the church. Scott's drawings too were considered to be more expensive and more elaborate than funds permitted. Drawings were then sought from Bombay-based architects, in the hope that their plans would be more economical and have the additional advantage of providing supervision of the project on site.[12]

Bartle Frere had often criticised the lack of architectural elegance in British India. He felt strongly about the 'utter absence of anything like distinctive features', and despaired that early British administrators had 'left no good architecture behind them in India'. The building of the Afghan Church offered a valuable opportunity to build the first 'ecclesiologically pure' church in India, one which would celebrate a Christian vision. Frere intended the Memorial Church to be a harbinger of change, built in the Gothic style and to be emulated widely.[13]

The commission to build the Afghan Church was won in 1847 by Welsh hydraulic engineer and amateur architect Henry Conybeare, who had recently arrived in Bombay to work on surveys required for the construction of the Great

Fig 8.5 | Church of St. John the Evangelist, Colaba, Mumbai, also known as the Afghan Memorial Church (1847–58), by Henry Conybeare. This church was the first building to be built in the Gothic Revival style in western India using local Kurla and Gujarat Porbunder stone. The spire was added in 1865 [Victorian and Albert Museum, London].

Fig 8.6 | Interior of the Church of St. John the Evangelist [Hersh Acharya].

Indian Peninsula Railway. Conybeare (1823–84) was the son of William Daniel Conybeare, a well-known geologist and Dean of Llandaff Cathedral in Cardiff, Wales. As Dean of Llandaff, William had initiated and supervised large-scale restoration work on the Cathedral. It is very likely that Henry Conybeare's life-long interest in Gothic architecture stemmed from these early years, having witnessed first-hand a major restoration project. The family was deeply religious, for his brother Charles Ranken Conybeare, also joined the church and served as Vicar of St Mary's Church at Itchenstoke in Aylesbury, Hampshire. When the rebuilding of St Mary's Church was undertaken in 1868, it was done so on the basis of drawings provided by Henry Conybeare.

It is possible that being fellow ecclesiologists, and each deeply committed to the Gothic cause, Henry Conybeare, Bartle Frere and George Gilbert Scott knew each other. It is also possible that Conybeare's decision to come out to India in search of work was at the suggestion of Bartle Frere. More needs to be researched on the long-term impact of these interactions and the transmission of knowledge across countries and cultures.

Conybeare's drawings for the Church of St John the Evangelist were strongly recommended by Rev. George Pigott to his colleagues. Pigott referred to them as being 'in the Gothic or rather Christian style of architecture'. Approved by the Committee, construction work on the Church of St John the Evangelist (Afghan Memorial Church) was began in 1847. The building was completed ten years later and the Church consecrated by Bishop Harding and opened to the congregation on 7 January 1858 [fig. 8.6]. General Fuller supervised and ensured its completion after Conybeare was appointed Superintendent of Repairs to the newly constituted Board of Conservancy in 1848 and placed on special duty for the construction of the Vihar Water Works in 1852.[14] A 65 ft spire was added to the church later, in 1865.[15]

The late-1850s were turbulent years that witnessed the Great Rebellion against British rule and the Indian rural elite in large parts of the Indian sub-continent. Though the rebellion's epicentre lay in the Meerut, Delhi, Saharanpur, and Kanpur districts of north India, news of growing support for the rebellion in Bombay town and Presidency reached the Bombay Government. Tales of violence unnerved many and rumours heightened fear. Even the most distinguished succumbed. Secretary James Lumsden feared for his life and slept on board a ship docked in Bombay harbour. Dr George Buist, leading intellectual and editor of the *Bombay Times*, wrote vitriolic pieces against the rebels to which the paper's Indian proprietors reacted sharply and Buist lost his job. To the beleaguered British, their places of Christian worship such as the Afghan Church and St Thomas's Cathedral in Bombay and churches elsewhere, offered refuge and solace.[16]

ARCHITECTURAL FEATURES OF THE AFGHAN CHURCH

The Afghan Church represents 'a milestone' in the history of ecclesiastical architecture in India, states Dwivedi

> *Until then, churches in the country were built in rubble and brick with a surface finish of smooth chunam or lime plaster. The Afghan Church was the first to be built with local stone – the walls of rubble with an exterior facing of coarse Kurla stone with coigns, arches, piers, and carvings in beige Porbunder stone.*[17]

It was the interior of the Afghan Church that made it special. The chancel floor, observes Dwivedi, was lined with English tiles on patterns provided by William Butterfield. Excellent craftsmanship from the Lockwood Kipling School of Art (today known as the J.J. School of Art) provided the intricate and beautiful metal screen. Metal screens were accorded a special place in Gothic Revival architecture and were strongly advocated by Pugin. Names of the many soldiers and commissioned officers who had died and the regiments to which they belonged were inscribed. Their heroism and sacrifice was not to be forgotten. A poignant inscription on the walls of the church read:

This church was built in memory of the officers whose names are written above, and of the non-commissioned officers and private soldiers, too many to be recorded, who fell, mindful of their duty, by sickness or by the sword, in the campaigns of Sind and Afghanistan, 1835–43 AD

One of the eight bells placed in the tower of the Church 'spelt out a clear message: "Tell it out among the heathen that the Lord is King".'[18]

Beautiful stained glass was an important and integral feature of the Afghan Church. Forty-two panels were imported from Britain from the ateliers of well-known stained glass artists, such as William Wailes, who had designed them. As with stained glass elsewhere, these had biblical themes to provide visual education and convey the message of the Gospel more effectively to the congregation. Among the themes and stories were those of the prophets Abraham and Isaac, of the Crucifixion and of 'Our Lord in Majesty and Power'.[19]

When completed, the Church of St John the Evangelist received a mixed response. Some commented that though the materials used were not of the best quality, the general effect was 'extremely good and [the] appearance of richness has been obtained with considerable skill'. Others noted that, though not architecturally outstanding, the Afghan Church was important for being among the first Gothic Revival churches to be built in British India on principles laid down by the Ecclesiological Society. Conybeare's designs for the Afghan Church initiated a style which would dominate the architectural landscape of Bombay city for more than half a century.

BRITISH INDIA'S FIRST URBAN PLANNER

More research is needed on the life of Henry Conybeare, who has claim to being British India's first urban planner. Like many of his eminent contemporaries in Victorian Britain, sanitary reformers such as Edwin Chadwick, John Simon and William Farr, Conybeare saw the sacred in the secular and championed the cause of civic reform and urban planning. The sanitary reformers viewed themselves as missionaries engaged in preaching the 'Civic Gospel', advocating the connection between 'Cleanliness' and 'Godliness' in the public health movement. What was applicable to industrialised Britain was also seen to hold true for the colonies.[20]

Conybeare strongly advocated comprehensive urban planning, being acutely conscious of the interdependence of every aspect of the city's infrastructure. Be it water supply, sanitation, drainage, building legislation, municipal taxation or architecture, each required synchronisation with the other. This, he believed, was essential for the health, economic prosperity, and well-being of the city's inhabitants. Like his peers he recognised the importance of the municipal engineer, who like the family physician, was concerned with every aspect of the city's health and well-being.

In an age when disciplines were not water-tight, it was possible for a hydraulic engineer to undertake architectural and civic infrastructural projects. At his most expansive, Henry Conybeare visualised the laying down of a system, a master plan, for the setting up of public works and civic infrastructural projects in British India and other British colonies.[21] However, differences with the Bombay Government led to Conybeare's resignation in 1856 while on deputation to Britain to finalize plans for the Vihar Water Works. He objected to the Bombay Government beginning work on the project without his water plans having been finalized. The Bombay Government justified its actions on the grounds of a severe water shortage that occurred in Bombay during the years 1853–55 which posed a serious threat to the lives of Bombay's inhabitants. Water had to be procured somehow and work at Vihar was started with incomplete plans. In July 1856 Henry Conybeare submitted his resignation to the Bombay authorities stating:

> *I therefore only regret that the works should have been commenced when*
> *they were because as an Engineer I well know that time is generally lost*
> *in the end by being in too great a hurry to commence an important task.*[22]

After his resignation, Conybeare continued to be involved with improvements in public works projects in India and taught civil engineering at Chatham where junior officers of the Royal and East India Company Engineers were sent to be trained. But it was to church building and railway projects that he devoted much of his time. He published what he hoped would be the first of five volumes on the all-important subject of principles governing Gothic Revival architecture entitled, *The Ten Canons of Proportion and Composition in Gothic Architecture ...and Practically Applied to the Design of Modern Churches* (1868). It was illustrated mainly with his own designs, and the book was privately published.[23] The other four volumes were never published, for the book failed to make a mark. Critics termed it 'ramshackle but scholarly'. By a strict adherence to Gothic architectural principles, Conybeare had hoped to bring Church building 'under the reign of law'. Some critics referred to his 'passionate, eccentric interest in Gothic architecture and the problems of modern Church building', but did not think too highly of his architectural abilities. Being the recipient of bad press was not new to Conybeare. On his many confrontations with leading members of Bombay's merchant community, such as Jamsetjee Jejeebhoy and Mohammed Ali Roghay, as well as the general public, Lord John Elphinstone, Governor of Bombay, had wryly commented: 'because he is a hydraulic engineer, Henry Conybeare has the habit of getting into hot water.'[24]

Among Conybeare's important contributions in Britain was his building of the church of St Patrick on Cromwell Road, London. Conybeare's association with Samuel Charles Haines, Vicar of St Mathias led him to prepare designs for the renovation of the church of St Mathias. These designs were shown at the Royal Academy and were published in the *Building News*. Conybeare intended St Patrick's to be special and based his designs on an early Gothic style termed 'Rhenish Romanesque'.[25]

Considerable effort went into planning a tall campanile with a prominent bell-stage for this church, which was to have 'a first-class peal of eight, similar to Mr Denison's at Doncaster'. The church bells were to swing freely and chime out what Conybeare hoped would be melodic notes from the most beautiful of Schubert's songs. The plans for St Patrick's resembled designs which he had prepared some years earlier for the Holy Trinity Church at Dorchester. These designs were included in his book. However, a number of architectural features which Conybeare hoped to incorporate in the church of St Patrick were not implemented due to lack of funds. When completed in 1879, it was praised in the *Kensington News* for 'its blue-painted walls, its harmonious features, its ... bell-pull and pretty "baby-like" font'.[26] Among Conybeare's drawings for several other Gothic Revival churches, only one, a 'small but competent and very French example' at Itchen Stoke, Aylesbury, in Hampshire (1866), was actually built. It was here that his brother Charles Ranken Conybeare served as Vicar.[27]

Conybeare set up an engineering company in London along with Mr Percy. They prepared plans for railway construction in Wales. Drawings were submitted for building the railroad known as St John the Evangelist Brecon Section and the St John the Evangelist and Llandingad Section in 1860–61. At the time railways were being built in Wales, especially by the Brecon and Llandovery Railway Company in Carmarthenshire. In 1878, Conybeare emigrated to Caracas, Venezuela, and died there a few years later. Little is known of his reasons for emigrating or of the work that he wished to accomplish there. The date of his death is disputed with some reports stating 1884 and others 1892.

FRERE TOWN AND GOTHIC REVIVAL ARCHITECTURE IN LATE-NINETEENTH-CENTURY BOMBAY

Plans for forty buildings were drawn up by James Trubshawe, architect to the Esplanade Fee Committee, the body constituted to design and oversee the building of the new central business district in Bombay in the 1860s. Trubshawe drew heavily on Professor T.R. Smith's recommendations. Smith, an influential member of the Architectural Association in London, took a keen interest in buildings – both domestic and public – in British India.

Prominent among the impressive public buildings built in these decades were the Public Works Secretariat (1872), the Government Secretariat (1874), the University buildings (1874) [fig.s 8.1, 8.4], the High Court (1878), the General Post Office (1874) and the Telegraph Office (1874).[28] They were planned along the Esplanade together with the David Sassoon Mechanics' Institute (1870), the Elphinstone College (1871) [fig. 8.7] and the Royal Alfred Sailors' Home (1876). Using local Kurla and Porbunder stone, with a blend of Gothic and Indian architecture, they bore testimony to the power and confidence of the Victorian colonial state in the later years of the nineteenth century.[29]

By the beginning of the twentieth century the Gothic Revival had been replaced by the so-called Indo-Saracenic style. Examples of the Indo-Saracenic include George Wittet's design for the Gateway of India [fig. 8.8], commemorating the visit of King George V and Queen Mary in 1911, and the Prince of Wales Museum in the Fort area of South Bombay. Wittet also planned the Ballard Estate

Fig 8.7 | Elphinstone College (*left*) and the David Sassoon Mechanics Institute (*right*), Hornby Road, 'Frere Town'. The College was designed by James Trubshawe and completed by government engineer John Adams in 1888, while the Mechanics Institute was designed by Scott, McClelland & Co. and completed in 1870 [Farooq Issa, *Phillips Images*, Mumbai].

Fig 8.8 | The Gateway of India, Apollo Bunder, Colaba, Mumbai (1914–24), by George Wittet [Farooq Issa, *Phillips Images*, Mumbai].

Scheme that laid down guidelines for the development of the northern part of the Central Business District [fig. 8.9].[30] The 1930s saw the emergence of the 'Bombay' or 'Nationalist School of Architecture' that gained prominence in the subsequent decade. Architects expressed concern about the state of the built environment in promoting the well-being of Bombay's inhabitants. Professor Claude Batley was foremost among twentieth century architects who emphasised the importance of architecture to social well-being.

Fig 8.9 | The new central business district of Bombay known as the Ballard Estate (1908–14), by George Wittet [Farooq Issa, *Phillips Images,* Mumbai].

For Batley, as for his predecessors, such as Henry Conybeare and Bartle Frere, city planning had to take place in a comprehensive manner. Each part impacted upon the whole. 'For Claude Batley as for nineteenth century civic reformers who preached "the civic Gospel", and strove to educate the public on the connections between cleanliness and godliness, civic and moral life, the sacred and the secular were intertwined. In short, a religiosity pervaded all understanding of the built form, for in the last analysis God was the ultimate architect, and the Kingdom of God the ultimate city.'[31]

In the 1990s, need for major restoration work on the Church led to the coming together of the church authorities and a citizens' group known as "Friends of the Afghan Church", that emphasised the importance of the Church of St John the Evangelist (or Afghan Church) in Mumbai's social and architectural history. Press coverage brought the church considerable public attention. This, however, was short lived. Today, the Afghan Church has once again faded into the background, and needs, like so many other historic Gothic Revival structures of post-colonial Mumbai, to be integrated, albeit on different terms into the city's cultural and religious life and recognised as a valued part of the city's heritage.

NOTES

1. See T.R. Metcalf, *An Imperial Vision: Indian Architecture and Britain's Raj*, London, 1989; G. Stamp, 'Victorian Bombay: Urbs Primus in India', *Art & Archaeology Research Papers*, no. 2 (1977); and J. Morris and S. Winchester, *Stones of the Empire*, Oxford, 1983.

2. Maharashtra State Archives (hereafter MSA), Mumbai, Ecclesiastical Department, vol. 3, 1847; A.J. Nix-Seamen, *The Afghan War Memorial Church and Historical Notes on Colaba*, Bombay, 1938; H.E. Cox, *The Story of St Thomas' Cathedral, Bombay*, Bombay, 1946.

3. C.W. London, *Bombay Gothic*, Mumbai, 2002.

4. *Ibid*. See also C. W. London, 'Architect of Bombay's Hallmark Style: Stevens and the Gothic Revival', in P. Rohatgi, P. Godrej, and R. Mehrotra (eds.), *Bombay to Mumbai Changing Perspectives*, Mumbai, 1997, pp.236–49.

5. M. Dossal, *Theatre of Conflict, City of Hope: Bombay c. 1661 to Present Times,* Oxford, 2010, pp.184–94.

6. Nix-Seamen, *op. cit.* [note 2], p.1.

7. Henry Moses cited in S. Dwivedi and R. Mehrotra, *Bombay: The Cities Within*, Mumbai, 1995, p.66.

8. Nix-Seamen, *op. cit.* [note 2], p.2–4.

9. S. Dwivedi, 'Christian Churches', in *Bombay To Mumbai Changing Perspectives*, Mumbai, 1997, pp.189–90. See also correspondence between The Rev George Pigott and the Bombay Government on the building of the Church of St John the Evangelist, MSA, GD, vol. 20, 1843.

10. J. Holliday, '19th-Century Stained Glass in Bombay: Its Role in the Architectural and Ideological Landscape', unpublished PhD Thesis (University of Mumbai), 2001, p.16. See also G. Kitson Clark, *The Making of Victorian England*, New York, 1976, pp.169–73.

11. *Ibid*. (Holliday), p,19.

12. *Ibid*., pp.17–19.

13. London, *op. cit.* [note 3], pp.16–18. Unfortunately, George Gilbert Scott's drawings for the Afghan Memorial Church were lost, perhaps in the shipwreck that destroyed Bartle Frere's private papers and other personal belongings.

14. M. Dossal, 'Henry Conybeare and the Politics of Centralized Water Supply in Mid-Nineteenth Century Bombay', *The Indian Economic and Social History Review*, vol. 25:1 (1988), pp.79–96.

15. Dwivedi, *op. cit.* [note 9], p.191

16. M. Dossal, *Imperial Designs and Indian Realities:The Planning of Bombay City 1845–1875*, Oxford, 1991, pp.47 – 52. See also Eric Stokes, *The Peasant Armed: The Indian Revolt of 1857*, Oxford, Clarendon Press, 1986.

17. Dwivedi, *op. cit.* [note 9], p.191.

18. London, *op., cit.* [note 3], pp.17–18, and Nix-Seamen, *op cit.* [note 6].

19. London, *ibid*., p.17.

20. Dossal, *op. cit.* [note 16], pp.110–14.

21. *Ibid*.

22. *Ibid*.

23. Holliday, *op. cit.* [note 10], p.67.

24. Dossal, *op. cit.* [note 16].

25. British History Online (www.british-history.ac.uk) 'Survey of London: volume 42: Kensington Square to Earl's Court'.

26. *Ibid*.

27. *Ibid*.

28. Recent research has shown that architects other than George Gilbert Scott played a leading role in the design and construction of the University of Bombay buildings. See Richard Butler, 'George Gilbert Scott and the University of Bombay', *The Victorian*, no. 37, 2011, pp.10–13.

29. Dossal, *op. cit.* [note 5], pp.146–8.

30. Metcalf, *op. cit.* [note 1], pp.94–8.

31. Dossal, *op.cit.* [note 5], pp.184–91.

9 · Churches of the Holy Zebra: the Technicolor Meeting House in North America

MICHAEL J. LEWIS

One can date precisely the arrival of High Victorian architecture in the United States: on 8 July, 1853, the trustees of All Souls, Unitarian, having purchased a lot at Fourth Avenue and Twentieth Street, New York, examined plans for a cruciform church in the Lombard style. The distinguished minister of the congregation, the Rev. Henry W. Bellows, was chary of both design and designer, twenty-eight year old Jacob Wrey Mould. But both were pushed forward by his wealthiest trustee, Moses H. Grinnell, who would contribute the lion's share of the cost of construction. The Rev. Bellows suspected that Grinnell was 'bewitched by the architect', but gave his approval.[1] Some two years later, on 25 December 1855, the church opened, to the acute bafflement of the public [fig. 9.2]. In a country with no tradition of structural polychromy, Mould drenched his walls in lurid colour, vibrant bands of creamy Caen stone, imported from France, alternating with bright red Philadelphia pressed brick, and columns of green, blue and mottled marble. It was easily, one critic noted, 'the most violent contrast that our building materials afford'.[2] The distressingly strident building prompted countless ribald epithets, some of which survive: 'Immaculate Beef-steak', 'Joseph's Coat', 'Fat and Lean' and 'Holy Zebra'.[3] Yet knowledgeable critics at once saw it as a building of immense consequence. *The Crayon*, America's most influential art journal, pronounced it 'a work of merit and genius, second to none in our city'.[4] And the Ruskinian *New Path* praised it as a 'very excellent edifice [that should be] the subject of careful study both by the architect and the amateur'.[5]

All Souls has long been recognised as a central building of the American Gothic Revival, but it is a curious fact that no-one has thought to ask how it came to be built by Unitarians.[6] After all, High Victorian architecture emerged largely as a result of the Oxford movement, championed by the Ecclesiological Society through the revival of Catholic ritual and art within the Anglican Church. Its first great building, All Saints, Margaret Street (1849–59), was funded by A.J.B. Beresford Hope, that staunch defender of the High Church cause.[7] But Unitarians were dissenters from orthodoxy, and resolutely so. The most liberal of protestant denominations, they were deeply sceptical toward ritual, believing that every article of faith must be rigorously subjected to reason. That the same architectural imagery could be embraced by two religious bodies that were diametrically opposed in so many things poses a problem of interpretation. Either the forms of High Victorian architecture meant nothing – and were mere fashionable

Fig 9.2 | All Souls Unitarian Church, New York (1853–5), by Jacob Wrey Mould.

haberdashery, to be used by all denominations – or else they did indeed mean something, but something that exercised peculiar appeal to either of the ends of the High Church/Low Church spectrum. If this is the case, and I believe it is, High Victorian architecture played a strangely variable part in the intricate negotiation of style that preoccupied every religious denomination in the middle decades of the nineteenth century.

There is no mystery why the architect of All Souls was drawn to colour; he had been thinking about it for the whole of his professional life. Jacob Wrey Mould was born in England in 1825, studied at King's College, London, and upon graduation in 1839 was articled as an apprentice to that great theorist of architectural colour, Owen Jones. He assisted Jones with his two pioneering works of chromolithography, *The Alhambra* (for which he 'executed with his own hands, from casts or from Mr Jones's sketches, illustrations of the second volume') and the *Grammar of Ornament*.[8] Mould completed his apprenticeship in 1849, worked briefly for Lewis Vuliamy, but returned to Jones to work on the vibrant colour scheme of the Crystal Palace.[9] When New York built its own Crystal Palace in

Fig 9.3 | Rectory of All Souls.

Fig 9.4 | All Souls Unitarian, original design with campanile.

1853, he came to advise its architects on colour. One sees why Mould liked to brag, in his most quoted remark, 'I'm hell on color'.[10]

In our own generation, computer-assisted renderings have had a transformative effect on architecture, first changing how a building could be depicted, and then changing public expectations as to what a finished building should look like. Something similar happened in Jones and Mould's generation. The chromolithographs they made were the first prints to approach the full intensity of spectral colour, i.e., that of sunlight passed through a prism. One could now capture the entire range of architectural colour with great fidelity. But with All Souls, one has the sense that Mould tried to reverse the process, and to make a building that was as bright as a chromolithograph. One wonders if it was the startling intensity of his presentation drawings that mesmerised his clients.

And not merely his clients. Two students at New York's Free Academy, Peter Bonnet Wight and Russell Sturgis, were so overwhelmed by the sight of Mould's drawings that they decided on the spot to become architects, later becoming key figures in the High Victorian movement. Over fifty years later, Wight could still

Fig 9.5 | Interior of All Souls, Unitarian Church, New York (1853–5).

summon the thrill of seeing Mould's work: 'such drawings! I have never seen better since. Everything was drawn in ink and coloured on fine white drawing paper, backed with muslin.'[11] They do not survive, alas, but by extrapolating from Wight's imitations we can get a sense of their vibrancy [fig. 9.1].

Equally bold was Mould's sense of form. Although he drew his motifs from Lombard buildings, including San Zeno Maggiore in Verona, he used them in a fresh and spirited way. He did not anchor his design in pyramidal fashion on his central cupola – the conventional solution – but flung his boldest forms to the margins of his composition, recalling that tendency of contemporary German *Rundbogenstil* to accentuate the periphery. At the rear of the building he placed a gloriously overwrought parish house, which thrust its second story bay forward on immensely exaggerated brackets that reached almost to the ground [fig. 9.3]. At the adjacent corner would have been his most dynamic form, a corner campanile that would have risen 227ft to flare outwards into a fiercely machicolated belfry [fig. 9.4].[12] But it was never built, to the great detriment of the building, for it was – as a fellow architect put it – 'the bass-note necessary to complete the harmonious chord'.[13]

Only in the interior was the specifically Unitarian character of the building apparent. A broad auditorium-like space, with short stubby arms and a mere niche of an apse, it was essentially a preaching box and it recalled the colonial meeting houses in which their Puritan forebears had worshipped. Above was an open timber truss with trefoil ornament, an incongruous Gothic feature explicable only as a concession to that High Victorian insistence on structural truth [fig. 9.5]. In its original form, it was even more clearly an auditorium. Behind the pulpit, the Rev. Bellows installed an eight-foot 'paraboloid', a sounding board in the form of a shell with a decidedly Unitarian purpose: 'for increasing the power of the speaker's voice'.[14]

At first glance, the swift transmission of High Victorian architecture from London to New York seems utterly unremarkable. English periodicals brought images of newly constructed buildings, as did a steady stream of English architects who sought their fortune in North America (besides Mould, there was Richard Upjohn, Frank Wills, Joseph C. Wells, Gervase Wheeler, Frederick Clark Withers, Calvert Vaux, and many more). But they came from a culture where the Gothic Revival was dominated by High Anglican interests. To be sure, the two most famous figures of the Gothic Revival were not themselves High Anglican: A.W.N. Pugin was a Roman Catholic convert and John Ruskin an evangelical. Nevertheless, the movement itself was broadly and comprehensively Anglican. It was in Anglican church building that its formal advances took place and in Anglican intellectual circles, particularly the Ecclesiological Society, where its theoretical life was centred. The crusade for archaeological rectitude in the 1840s was essentially an Anglican phenomenon, culminating in 1844 when *The Ecclesiologist* enjoined architects to reject invention and to build scrupulously accurate replicas of Early Middle-Pointed churches. And All Saints Margaret Street, the church that spectacularly upended the archaeological interlude, was a prestigious Anglican project.

The English model applies neatly to Canada, where English émigrés such as Frank Wills carried with them a faithful version of Ecclesiological doctrine. But the situation in the United States was thoroughly different. The Episcopal Church, the counterpart to the Church of England, enjoyed no privileged status and in any event made up a tiny fraction of the population. By 1886, for example, there were twenty times as many Roman Catholics, ten times as many Methodists, seven times as many Baptists, and nearly three times as many Lutherans and Presbyterians; Episcopalians represented fewer than two percent of the population.[15] While Roman Catholics were the single largest denomination, the vast majority of American churchgoers attended Low Church protestant denominations. Thus the cultural substrate – the belief system that determined the national mood – was not Anglican, and had no particular reverence for the Church of England, in either its crypto-Catholic or Broad Church establishment mood. This fact has never been sufficiently recognised in the scholarly literature on the American Gothic Revival, which has generally relied on the English historiography that is so useful in understanding Episcopalian architecture and so deceiving when applied to other denominations.

These Low Church and dissenting denominations viewed the Gothic Revival with a mixture of fascination and suspicion. They may have enjoyed Gothic literature, admired Walter Scott's Waverly novels, and collected prints of romantic Gothic ruins along the Rhine, but they had no interest in building a fully-developed Gothic church like New York's Trinity Church (1841–46). A generic medievalism was fashionable, but a specifically Catholic one was not. Here the Romanesque offered a welcome compromise: there was a tasteful medievalism, but no frenzied play of finials and spires that hinted at mysticism, only a few stylistic cues such as pilaster strips and a corbel table frieze.[16] The resulting building presented a compact and sober volume, vaguely suggestive of a meeting house. This was the preferred solution of American Congregationalists, who gave the style official approval when they published *A Book of Plans for Churches and Parsonages* (1853).[17] The great advantage of the Romanesque was elasticity; it could be inflected to make an archaeologically plausible Norman Romanesque (for Episcopalians who stressed their Englishness) to a bitingly modern German *Rundbogenstil* (for Lutherans who stressed their Germanness or Calvinists their modernity).[18]

Unitarians stood apart from this general pattern, and from the moment of their ascendance in 1805, which marked their formal break with New England Congregationalism, they made free use of the Gothic.[19] But this was an older variant, not the rapturously medieval Gothic of the Ecclesiological Society, but the self-consciously literary Gothic of Horace Walpole or Walter Scott. Its pedigree reached back into the eighteenth century, where it stood archly aloof from the Georgian context, and the very last thing it sought was the revival of medieval ritual or social organisation. In short, it was the architectural language of cultured Nonconformity.

This mysticism-free Gothic resulted in buildings like Bowdoin Street Chapel in Boston (1831), designed by Solomon Willard. Though executed in robust local granite, it might as well have been built of boards, so paper-thin were its crenellations, pointed arches, and quatrefoils – garnishes applied to a classical box. Even the gabled roof was suppressed, concealed behind the parapet to produce an image of stereometric clarity [fig. 9.6]. And yet the Bowdoin Street Chapel became the normative model for Unitarian churches, especially in New York, where several major churches were soon built (outside of New England, where they could take over existing Puritan houses of worship, Unitarians had to build anew). The first, the Church of the Messiah at Waverly Place (1838), scrupulously followed the model of the Bowdoin Street Chapel: there was the same crenellated body of the church, the blocky central tower, also crenellated, and fronted with the same trio of Tudor arches below, an oculus above, and a traceried window between [fig. 9.7].

Although this boxy Gothic would gradually become more archaeologically accurate, its fundamentally intellectual and literary character would remain. So

Fig 9.6 | Bowdoin St. Church, Boston (1831), by Solomon Willard.

Fig 9.7 | Church of the Messiah, Waverly Place, New York (1838).

we see in the Church of the Saviour in Brooklyn, the creation of the Rev. Orville Dewey (1794–1882). When Dewey visited Europe in 1833, it was not the great cathedrals that pitched him into ecstasy but 'that abode of departed genius', Walter Scott's Abbotsford. 'I have seen it all – I have seen it!' he twice proclaimed in his diary.[20] At the same time, Dewey acquired what earlier Unitarian patrons had not had, which was a cultivated traveller's personal experience of genuine medieval architecture. Already he was thinking of applying its lessons to a church of his own, as his comments following a visit to York Minster reveal:

> I confess that if I could build a church in all respects to suit my own taste, I would build it in the solemn and beautiful style of the churches of England, the Gothic style; and I would build it in enduring stone, that it might gather successive generations within its holy walls, that passing centuries might shed their hallowing charm around it.[21]

Indeed he did, building his Church of the Savior emphatically in stone, although the result had as much in common with Abbotsford as York.

To design the Church of the Savior (1842–44), Dewey turned to the only Unitarian architect then at work in New York, Minard Lafever, who obliged him with a lively performance in the Perpendicular Gothic [fig. 9.10].[22] The church was a high-gabled volume, vigorously crenellated but lacking a central tower; instead, its vertical theme was stated in the octagonal spires that flanked the central bay and shot high above the roofline. Unlike the schematic Gothic of the Bowdoin Street Chapel, it was historically plausible, and one can imagine the portfolios of John Britton and John Milner were not far from Lafever's drawing board. At the same time, there was no theological conviction in its use of the Gothic: no attempt to link the building to the piety of the High Middle Ages, no invocation of the Gothic as the sign of a specific social and religious order. While Richard Upjohn's contemporary Trinity Episcopal Church (1841–46) worked very hard to look as if it were built in the fourteenth century, one has the sense that the Church of the Savior was content to look like a plate from Britton's *Architectural Antiquities of Great Britain*. It is this distinct bookishness that places the building in the older literary tradition of the Gothic, which was the marker of an independent intellectual disposition. It flaunted rather than concealed its modernity, even in the way that its slender spires terminated in prominent lightning rods rather than crosses. For this reason the Rev. Dewey was careful to call his building "semi-Gothic".

Such was the architectural tradition – highly literary, proudly Nonconformist and (in its view of the Gothic) self-consciously modern rather than nostalgic or sentimental – that the Rev. Bellows called upon when he came to build All Souls, Unitarian.

Henry Whitney Bellows (1814–1882) was one of America's most famous clergymen. After graduating from Harvard College and Harvard Divinity School, he became pastor of New York's First Unitarian Church in 1839, an appointment he held until his death. He seems to have been inexhaustible. He edited *The Christian*

Inquirer and *The Christian Examiner*, helped to establish Cooper Union (together with his friend and congregant Peter Cooper), and from 1861 to 1878 presided over the United States Sanitary Commission – the Civil War institution that was the forerunner of the Red Cross. In every respect, he was a central figure of American cultural and intellectual life.

Before he built All Souls, Bellows had already commissioned a church, the Church of the Divine Unity, which stood on Broadway near Prince Street. Like many novice patrons, he moved cautiously in his first effort, deferring to Dewey in the choice of both style and architect.[23] He employed Lafever, who cleverly paraphrased his own Church of the Messiah, eliminating the side bays to fit the narrower site while swelling the entrance arch into a voluptuous ogee [fig. 9.8]. The new church was dedicated on Christmas Day, 1845, with a sermon by the Rev. William Henry Furness, the father of the architect Frank Furness.[24]

But in one respect, Bellows stands out as a bold patron, and that is in his frank acceptance of the facts of the contemporary world – the realities of real estate, land values and even the visual demands of a modern commercial street. Because of the high cost of land on Broadway, the building committee could only purchase thirty feet of frontage, which gave him little more than the width of a townhouse (the lot widened somewhat at the rear). Bellows made a virtue out of the narrow site and rather than build a dwarf church, he chose instead to build a colossal portal. His street front is all entrance, no wall, the imposing preface to something quite grand, rather than something squeezed and pinched.

Here Bellows proved himself even less of a historicist than Dewey. In his sermons he constantly stressed his openness to the pulsating energies of the modern world. He outraged his prudish fellow ministers by attending the theatre.[25] 'I know and confess myself to be a child of the age,' he proclaimed. 'Its peculiar ideas and characteristic emotions throb in my brain and tingle in my blood.'[26] But although he wrote prolifically, and often commented on architecture, he seems to have had little interest in the specifics of the historical styles. His two-volume account of his travels through Europe and Egypt is filled with perceptive remarks about buildings, but invariably about their function or character, never their stylistic pedigree. (His only reference to All Souls was a bemused remark that the striped buildings of Cairo reminded of it.[27]) His dedicatory sermon for All Souls is conspicuously free of stylistic terminology. Instead he explained it in terms of such rational principles as avoidance of ostentation and indifference to criticism:

> *It has been our conscientious aim to make a building in which mean economy, superficial show, worldly artifice and fraud, should not enter – a building religious in its structure, from cornerstone to dome; and if a consummate skill, an unfailing taste, an unsparing devotion, a self-possession which neither ridicule nor blame could disturb, and a zeal which neither sickness nor pain could impair – if these deserve fame, then indeed the modest architecture of this Christian temple has achieved it.*[28]

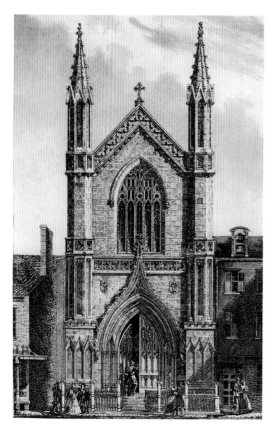

Fig 9.8 | Church of the Divine Unity, Broadway, New York (1845), by Minard Lafever.

Fig 9.9 | Lutheran Church of the Holy Communion, Philadelphia (1870–5), by Frank Furness and George Hewitt.

But Bellows' indifference to criticism does not mean that All Souls was merely an expression of intensely idiosyncratic personal taste. Bellows, perhaps more than any contemporary Unitarian thinker, recognised that religion is a collective enterprise, and cannot be purely personal. To the contrary, he believed that an excessive stress on individual reason had brought Unitarianism to the point of crisis. Radical transcendentalists, nourished on German biblical criticism, had come to disbelieve in miracles, to doubt the divinity of Christ, and to view all of ritual as nothing more than a superstitious magic show. Their answer was, to follow the dictates of one's own conscience, or as Emerson controversially put it in his celebrated Address at the Harvard Divinity School graduation, to 'go alone'.

For Bellows, this could have only one 'logical end [which] is the abandonment of the Church as an independent institution, the denial of Christianity as a supernatural revelation, and the extinction of worship as a separate interest.'[29] This was the dramatic formulation of *The Suspense of Faith*, his celebrated 1859 sermon which called for the strengthening of the church as an institution, rooted in history and symbols.[30] The sermon was fiercely criticised, for the mention of symbols seemed to challenge the Unitarian belief in the centrality of the spoken word, the instrument of reason. But as Bellows replied in a subsequent sermon,

Front Elevation—

Plan of gallery.

Location of organ

Gallery Plan

Fig 9.10 | Minard Lafever's design for the Church of the Savior, Broolyn (1842–4)
[Brooklyn Historical Society].

'words are not the only language. Actions, tones, circumstances, speak equally loud.'[31] Even metaphor might serve the function of the spoken word. Although he did not specifically mention All Souls in his sermon, he hardly needed to; critics inevitably associated his stress on symbolism with the devices and symbols of his church.[32]

It was precisely the modernity of Bellows – the flagrant modernity of his High Victorian church and the equally flagrant embrace of the social institutions of the modern world – that affronted his critics. The anonymous reviewer of the *United States Magazine* conflated the two, linking Bellows' vulgar building with his vulgar love of theatre. All Souls suggested the 'gaiety of an opera house, or the carousing of a drinking saloon, rather than the serene beauty of a temple'.[33] A minister might go to the theatre, the critic insisted, but only to reform it. And certainly the theatre was ripe for reform, he continued in a rather mad digression, attacking the recent performance of the play *Camille* for showing the interior of a tuberculosis ward: 'A cough cannot be brought within the range of art. It is simply disgusting.'

We can take this as the extent of protestant dismay over the Holy Zebra: to compare it to the dying cough of a victim of consumption. But the protest was in vain. Because of its social fashionability, its distinguished membership, its impeccable Calvinist pedigree and the national prominence of its pastor, All Souls exerted an extraordinary and almost instantaneous affect on the architecture of protestant America. It served to make the High Victorian acceptable, and in a way that no High Church model could. It pried High Victorian eclecticism from its identification with Anglo-Catholic ecclesiology, and made it acceptable for denominations of every stripe. It is a conspicuous though little noted fact that in most parts of the United States, the first thoroughly High Victorian churches were built for Low Church and dissenting congregations, and not Episcopalians. The first fully polychromatic church in the Hudson River Valley was a Dutch Reformed Church, designed by F.C. Withers at Fishkill Landing (now Beacon) in 1859.[34] The first in Philadelphia, Beth Eden Church (begun 1864), was built for a Baptist congregation.[35] And in Baltimore it was Grace Methodist Church, begun in 1865.[36] Few of these churches matched the sheer chromatic fury of Mould's design; nonetheless, All Souls had hugely expanded the radius of freedom within which they could build. One must concede that the High Victorian interlude in American Low Church and dissenting congregations was not an envious imitation of High Church fashion, but emerged at the other end of the denominational spectrum, and in many cases preceded it.

This would not have happened without the Unitarian architectural tradition, in which there survived an older strand of the Gothic Revival, an intellectual and bookish strand that was quite distinct from the Ecclesiology of the 1840s, with its characteristic blend of High Church theology, archaeology and social thought. It was this older strand to which Low Church congregations responded, although probably in most cases at an intuitive level. It also ensured that this non-Anglican High Victorian movement was not merely derivative – an imitation of fashionable new forms, but without any generative powers of its own – but was rich in ideas and consequences.

For the course of the American Gothic Revival, these consequences were immense. Among them were the two most influential architects of the next generation, H.H. Richardson (1838–1886) and Frank Furness (1839–1912), Unitarians whose careers began in New York and who each launched his practice with a Unitarian church.[37] Each began by working in a distinctively High Victorian mode, gradually working his way to a highly personal and rather abstract style – much influenced by the Gothic rationalism of Viollet-le-Duc – that served as the point of departure to the generation of early modern architects who would replace them. By contrast, their peers who worked in what might be called the Anglican High Victorian mode, men such as Vaux, Withers or Richard M. Upjohn, never could match the brio of their early work, their careers ending on a dying fall.

At one time, the youthful High Victorian essays with which Richardson and Furness began their careers seemed nothing more than a provincial reflection of English developments [fig. 9.9]. It now seems clear that these developments recoiled against the hardy independent tradition represented by the Rev. Bellows' technicolor meeting house on Fourth Avenue, a tradition that encouraged individualism, that did not wrap the Middle Ages in a veil of nostalgia and, above all, that had no great quarrel with modernity.

1. H.W. Henderson, *A Loiterer in New York: Discoveries Made by a Rambler through Obvious yet Unsought Highways and Byways*, New York, 1917, p.231.
2. Such was the verdict of *The New Path*, the pugnacious journal of the Association for the Advancement of Truth in Art that was founded to bring the ideas of Ruskin to an American audience. *The New Path*, vol. 1:6 (1863) quoted in *The Civil Engineer and Architects Journal*, vol. 26 (Nov. 1862), p.316.
3. *Ibid.*
4. 'The Church of All Souls', *The Crayon*, vol. 5:1 (1858), pp.20–2. Although unsigned, the review is known to have been written by Leopold Eidlitz. See Montgomery Schuyler, 'A Great American Architect: Leopold Eidlitz', *Architectural Record*, vol. 24:3 (1908), p.178.
5. *The New Path* (1863), see footnote 2
6. The principal study is David T. Van Zanten, 'Jacob Wrey Mould: Echoes of Owen Jones and the High Victorian Styles in New York, 1853–1865', *Journal of the Society of Architectural Historians*, vol. 28:1 (1869), pp.41–57.
7. So tradition-minded was Beresford Hope that he even opposed the Deceased Wife's Sister Bill – the humane law that finally made it legal for a widower to marry the sister of his deceased wife (he 'fought like a tiger' against it, as John Summerson reminds us). See John Summerson, *Heavenly Mansions*, New York, 1963, p.160.
8. H.T. Peck, editor-in-chief, *The International Cyclopaedia: a Compendium of Human Knowledge*, vol. 10, New York, 1892, p.254.
9. *Ibid.* During Vuliamy's illness, Mould is said to have 'designed and erected the beautiful mansion at Stanhope Gate, Hyde Park, London, on the site of the marquis of Hereford's *Gaunt House*'. Returning to Jones, he also took part 'in the construction and decoration of the Moresque-Turkish divan at Buckingham Palace'.
10. '[Leopold] Eidlitz is death on form; but I'm hell on color'. See Montgomery Schuyler, *op. cit.* [note 4], p.178.
11. See P.B. Wight, 'Reminiscences of Russell Sturgis', *Architectural Record*, vol. 26:1 (1909),

pp.46–7. Also see Sarah B. Landau, *P.B. Wight: Architect, Contractor and Critic, 1938–1925*, Chicago, 1981.
12. Van Zanten, *op. cit.* [note 6], p.47. On the other hand, the proposed height is also given as 285ft – one foot higher than the spire of Trinity Church, then the tallest building on Manhattan – but this seems unreliable. See 'Reminiscences of an Old New Yorker', by 'An Old Foot', *Frank Leslie's Sunday Magazine*, vol.10 (1881), p.633.
13. 'The Church of All Souls', *op. cit.* [note 4], pp.20–2. Some of the revelations in Eidlitz's review clearly come from Mould himself, such as the detail that the building committee eliminated 'some six or seven feet of the height of the wall in the original design', and that the architect's commission was 'little more than $2000' when he was entitled to $5000 (i.e., 5% of $100,000).
14. *Dwight's Journal of Music*, vol. 19:2 (1861), p.11.
15. In that year there were 338,333 Episcopalians out of total church and synagogue membership of about 17,200,000. See *Documents of the Senate of the State of New York*, vol. 3:42 (1887), p.110.
16. See Kathleen Curran, *The Romanesque Revival: Religion, Politics and Transnational Exchange*, University Park, 2003.
17. Twelve of its eighteen suggested designs were Romanesque or otherwise round-arched. See Central Committee, General Congregational Convention, *A Book of Plans for Churches and Parsonages*, New York, 1853; Gwen W. Steege, 'The Book of Plans and the Early Romanesque Revival in the United States: a Study in Architectural Patronage', *Journal of the Society of Architectural Historians*, vol. 46:3 (1987), pp.215–27.
18. For example, John Notman's St Clements (1855–1859) and Holy Trinity (1856–1859), both in Philadelphia. See Constance M. Greiff, *John Notman, Architect*, Philadelphia, 1979.
19. Of course, if one believed that classical architecture was the natural expression of intellectual clarity, and of a reason-based faith, one might build a smart Greek

temple, as the Rev. William Henry Furness in Philadelphia (1828), whose First Unitarian Church was designed by William Strickland.

20. *The Works of Orville Dewey*, London, 1844, p.615. Besides his theological tracts, Dewey was also an important writer on art and culture, and at a time when Hiram Powers' *Greek Slave* was creating controversy – it was made unwelcome in Cincinnati – it was Dewey who wrote an extraordinary pamphlet arguing for the essential morality of the work.

21. *Ibid.*, p.618.

22. Jacob Landy, *The Architecture of Minard Lafever*, New York and London, 1970, pp.87–104.

23. This commission was unrecorded in Landy's monograph. The attribution to Lafever is confirmed by Bellows' remarks at the twenty-fifth anniversary of the consecration of the Church of Savior (1844–1869), where he paid his respects to 'the deceased architect Mr Lafever, who was also the architect of my Church of the Divine Unity'. See *Unitarianism in Brooklyn. A Sermon Preached by A.P. Putnam. In the Church of the Savior, Brooklyn, N.Y., at the Commemorative Services Held April 25th, 1869*, New York, 1869, p.38.

24. *Universalist Union*, vol. 10 (1845), p.816.

25. In his love of the theatre, Bellows may have felt a kinship to Mould, who was a prolific author and translator of opera libretti.

26. Henry Whitney Bellows, *A Sequel to 'The Suspense of Faith'*, New York, 1859, p.42.

27. Henry Whitney Bellows, *The Old World in Its New Face: Impressions of Europe in 1867 and 1868*, vol. 2, New York, 1869, pp.119–20.

28. *New York Journal of Commerce*, 27 December 1855, as quoted in Van Zanten, *op. cit.* [note 6], p.41.

29. Henry Whitney Bellows, *The Suspense of Faith: An Address to the Alumni of the Divinity School of Harvard University, Cambridge, Mass., Given July 19, 1859*, New York, 1859, p.10.

30. For the importance and influence of *The Suspense of Faith*, see Christopher L. Walton, '"Words Are Not the Only Language": Henry Whitney Bellows's View of Scripture', *Philocrites*, 4 May 1997 (http://www.philocrites.com/archives/003143.html).

31. Henry Whitney Bellows, *Re-Statements of Christian Doctrine, in Twenty-five Sermons*, New York, 1860, p.37.

32. For example, *Dwight's Journal of Music, op. cit* [note 14].

33. 'All Souls, Unitarian', *U.S. Magazine*, vol. 4:4 (1857), pp.415–17.

34. Francis R. Kowsky, *The Architecture of Frederick Clarke Withers and the Progress of the Gothic Revival in America after 1850*, Middletown, Connecticut, 1980.

35. Sarah Bradford Landau, *Edward T. and William A. Potter: American Victorian Architects*, New York and London, 1979.

36. John Dorsey and James Dilts, *A Guide to Baltimore Architecture*, Centreville, 1973.

37. Furness was the son of the Rev. William Henry Furness, who was a lifelong friend of Bellows, and enjoying punning shamelessly on their names – on furnaces and bellows – whenever they were together. Frank Furness studied in New York from 1859 to 1861, the pupil of Richard Morris Hunt, and when he attended services (by all accounts it cannot have been often) it would have been at the church of his father's friend. Likewise Richardson, when he came to live in New York from 1865 to 1874, opened an office at 67 Broadway, and would have found Bellows' church the closest. See Michael J. Lewis, *Frank Furness: Architecture and the Violent Mind*, New York, 2001; James F. O'Gorman, *Living architecture: A biography of H.H. Richardson*, New York, 1997.

10 · Contributors

BRIAN ANDREWS is an architectural historian specialising in nineteenth- and early twentieth-century churches. His exhibition catalogue *Creating a Gothic Paradise: Pugin at the Antipodes* (2002) was the winner of the 2003 William M.B. Berger Prize for British Art History. He is Heritage Officer for the Archdiocese of Hobart and a director of the Australian Pugin Foundation.

ALEX BREMNER is senior lecturer in architectural history at the University of Edinburgh. He specialises in the history and theory of Victorian architecture, with a particular interest in British imperial and colonial architecture. His forthcoming book *Imperial Gothic: Religious Architecture and High Anglican Culture in the British Empire, c.1840–70* is to be published by Yale University Press in Spring 2013.

PETER COFFMAN studied for his PhD at Queen's University, Kingston, and is currently Assistant Professor at Carleton University in Ottawa where he is supervisor of the History and Theory of Architecture programme. He is president of the Society for the Study of Architecture in Canada and author of *Newfoundland Gothic* (2008).

MARIAM DOSSAL is an urban and maritime historian of modern India. Her books include *Theatre of Conflict, City of Hope: Mumbai 1660 to Present Times* (2010) and *Imperial Designs and Indian Realities: the Planning of Bombay City* (1991). She is keenly committed to Mumbai's heritage conservation.

GILL HUNTER is an independent scholar who has written extensively on the life and career of the nineteenth-century English architect William White. She is author of the book *William White: Pioneer Victorian Architect* (2010).

MICHAEL J. LEWIS teaches American art at Williams College, Massachusetts. His books include *Frank Furness: Architecture and the Violent Mind* (2001) and *The Gothic Revival* (2002). His *August Reichensperger: The Politics of the German Gothic Revival* (1993) received the Society of Architectural Historians' Alice Davis Hitchcock award for the best book of the year.

MILES LEWIS is an architectural historian with interests in the history of building technology as a cultural phenomenon, decorative forms in the Mediterranean and Near East, vernacular architecture, and the history of prefabrication. He is emeritus professor of architecture at the University of Melbourne, and a Fellow of the Australian Academy of Humanities.

IAN LOCHHEAD teaches art history at the University of Canterbury, Christchurch, New Zealand. He has written extensively on the history of New Zealand architecture. His book, *A Dream of Spires: Benjamin Mountfort and the Gothic Revival*, was published in 1999.

DESMOND MARTIN is retired Assistant Director of the National Monuments Council (South Africa). He has authored two books, *The Bishop's Churches* (2005) and *Walking Long Street, Cape Town* (2007). His PhD thesis (2002) focused on the church building programme of the first Anglican bishop of Cape Town, Robert Gray and his wife, Sophia.

THE VICTORIAN SOCIETY

The Victorian Society is the champion for Victorian and Edwardian buildings in England and Wales. Our aims are:

CONSERVING
To save Victorian and Edwardian buildings or groups of buildings of special architectural merit from needless destruction or disfigurement.

INVOLVING
To awaken public interest in, and appreciation of, the best of Victorian and Edwardian arts, architecture, crafts and design;

EDUCATING
To encourage the study of these and of related social history and to provide advice to owners and public authorities in regard to the preservation and repair of Victorian and Edwardian buildings and the uses to which they can, if necessary, be adapted

The aims are linked, and through involving and educating the public, we can increase the likelihood of conserving buildings. Victorian and Edwardian buildings are irreplaceable, cherished, diverse, beautiful, familiar and part of our everyday life.

They contribute overwhelmingly to the character of places people love and places where people live. They belong to all of us. Their owners are really only custodians for future generations. Victorian and Edwardian buildings are part of our collective memory, and central to how we see ourselves as individuals, communities and as a nation.

When decisions are taken which affect their future, the debate must be open and informed. We need to understand what is special about Victorian and Edwardian buildings and landscapes so that any necessary changes can be incorporated without damaging them forever.

We don't want to lose our past through ignorance.

That's where the Victorian Society comes in. As a reservoir of expertise, as energetic campaigners, and as a community organisation bringing together individuals from all round the country, we have helped people save the buildings they value. Sometimes it has been major national monuments such as the Albert Memorial in London or the Albert Dock in Liverpool, but more often nowadays it is local churches threatened with closure or good houses flattened to make way for undistinguished offices.